PLANNING
a course

The Complete Guide to Teaching a Course
Ian Forsyth, Alan Jolliffe and David Stevens

Planning a Course
Preparing a Course
Delivering a Course
Evaluating a Course

The Complete Guide to **TEACHING a COURSE**

PLANNING
a course

1

Practical
Strategies
for
Teachers,
Lecturers
and Trainers

**Ian Forsyth, Alan Jolliffe
and David Stevens**

Second Edition

**KOGAN
PAGE**

First published in 1995
Second edition 1999

Kogan Page Limited
120 Pentonville Road
London N1 9JN
UK

Stylus Publishing Inc.
22883 Quicksilver Drive
Sterling, VA 20166
USA

British Library Cataloguing in Publication Data

A CIP record for this book is available from the British Library.

ISBN 0 7494 2807 4

Typeset by Jean Cussons Typesetting, Diss, Norfolk
Printed and bound in Great Britain by Biddles Ltd, Guildford and King's Lynn

Contents

Introduction

WHAT IS THIS BOOK ALL ABOUT?

This book focuses on the systematic design and development of learning materials appropriate for use with a variety of learners in a variety of settings. This edition now includes a chapter on the writing of learning objectives and the development of test items, along with a discussion of copyright issues.

This book, the first in a series of four, describes the planning and design of learning materials from their logical beginnings to their conclusion. Implicit in this discussion is the understanding that a growing number of learning experiences are now available to the learner on their desktop via the World Wide Web (WWW) in a so-called virtual learning environment rather than the familiar, physical classroom environment.

As we are all aware, the WWW opens up the possibility of global learning events that can be accessed by learners at any time and in virtually any location as long as they have the connection to the Internet. Does this rapid movement toward global learning mean that we have to throw out our previous planning practices? No – on the contrary, the use of the computer has not, unlike early discussions on the matter, made our lives in the classroom any easier. Rather it has made them significantly more complex, making planning an even more important event in the preparation of learning materials.

The aim of this book is to help you make the right decisions about the learning materials of all kinds you have to develop to support a learning event that you or someone else will be facilitating. The event itself may last just one day, one semester or even longer. This book will help you answer questions such as 'I've been asked to teach this course, so where do I start?' or 'What will the learning materials that I have to develop look like?' or 'What kind of materials will the learners need, what should they look like and where can I get them?'

WHAT DOES EACH CHAPTER COVER?

Each chapter in the book describes in detail each of the tasks that you will need to consider if you are going to develop 'good' learning materials.

Chapter 1 looks at determining what tasks must be done to start the job of designing and developing learning materials and finding out who can best help you do those tasks.

Chapter 2 outlines an alternative to the standard method of gathering information about the materials you are going to develop. It describes the use of a pro-forma document that can help you save time completing the information gathering phase of the work and will provide the documentation you need to support the various educational decisions that you will have to make as you continue developing your learning materials.

Chapter 3 provides you with the basic information you will need to make the learning materials development process run smoothly. It describes the various tasks that should be carried out and how each of those tasks need to be placed into a time frame that reflects a typical duration for the project. The chapter also asks you to consider the human resource and financial support you will need to complete the project successfully.

Chapter 4 describes a methodology for the development of a learner profile that outlines what a learner should know after they have completed the course. This and the following chapter are designed to help you determine what the course will look like so the right learning materials can be developed.

Chapter 5 continues the discussion started in the previous chapter. The chapter describes how a sub-profile can be developed to help you and/or the materials development team better understand what has to be covered in each of the topics the learner has to learn.

Chapter 6 is a discussion regarding the development of learning objectives. Good learning materials development planning starts with the acquisition of a broad overview of the learning curriculum. The development of learner goals along with both general and specific learning objectives should then be based on that curriculum. The learning objectives then serve as a way of determining learner performance and assessment standards.

Chapter 7 describes three basic instructional methodologies available to the teacher or trainer in the classroom. The chapter provides details of the type of instructional materials that can be used to promote the kind of learning that needs to take place. The chapter is designed to complement the development of the profile and sub-profile described in Chapters 4 and 5 and the decisions you will have to make regarding what methodology and supporting materials are best suited to 'teach' that particular topic so learning can take place.

Chapter 8 discusses a methodology that you can use to help you make various educational decisions about the redesign and redevelopment of various learning materials. It also provides you with a description of the tasks that can be carried out at various stages of materials redesign.

Chapter 9 reflects on how learning materials might be evaluated to aid the learners so that both they and the teacher can determine how much learning has taken place. It reviews various evaluation strategies that can be used to aid the teacher and the developer of the materials (assuming they are different people) determine what materials and learning strategies may need to be revised.

Chapter 10 describes the development of both subjective and objective test items. Testing is a controlled procedure by which the performance of the learner can be sampled and evaluated against a standard. The chapter describes this process and provides examples of various types of test items.

Chapter 11 is an overview of some of the many copyright issues you will need to explore when writing your materials. Gathering together various materials for use as part of your 'set' of learning materials involves works created by others. This chapter will help you determine what you can and cannot use as part of your materials and suggests ways to obtain copyright permission.

The final chapter brings all the pieces together to help you get a complete picture of the process and procedures used in the systematic development of learning materials.

WHO SHOULD READ THIS BOOK?

The audience for this book includes many different people, such as the classroom teacher, the trainer, the training unit manager, the learning materials developer and the project manager who has been asked to co-ordinate the development of learning materials. This is a wide audience that some would possibly see as being too diverse, but the processes, procedures and outcomes or products described in each chapter are versatile enough to be adapted for use in a variety of situations from the school classroom to the video conference training seminar and the on-line classroom. The adaptability and applicability of the materials is only restricted by those who use them.

SOME ASSUMPTIONS

Some assumptions have been made about the reader. First, it is assumed that you want to develop your learning materials systematically and that you are comfortable with the process and procedures you have to undergo to develop learning materials in this way.

There is a certain hesitation to use the word 'systematic' as it has connotations for some teachers of a design and development procedure of a rigid pattern of development that has no shades of grey. Used here, however, systematic is defined as a well thought out plan of action that is not sporadic and recognizes that shades of grey are inevitable in the complex process of learning materials development.

The book is not written as a textbook to help you become an instructional designer but rather to provide you with a structure to design and develop sound learning materials for your learners more effectively. That being the case, you should also understand that while the procedures described in this book appear to be very rigid, they are written that way to help you develop your materials with a solid foundation of documentation.

It is also assumed that you understand that course documentation will not only allow you to make rational educational decisions about what is, or is not, needed with respect to what you are developing, it will also assist you in making decisions about the people you may need to get to help you, the time needed to complete the project and the money being spent.

Finally you should also understand that the course documentation will provide you with a foundation for both formative and summative evaluation and provide you with the basis for the redesign of the learning materials once they have outlived their usefulness.

For those of you starting out down the road of systematic learning materials design and for those of you that have walked down the road before, you will always find the process an interesting one. You will quickly realize, once you start, that you are not dealing with an exact science and the foundation that you are trying to build is the result of a somewhat elusive process. As you continue, however, you will find that the development of your learning materials is both fluid and dynamic, constantly changing, constantly shifting (that's why you need a solid foundation!), often frustrating, but in the end, always a great deal of fun. Good luck!

Ian R. Forsyth
Alan K. Jolliffe
David I. Stevens

Chapter 1
Where Do I Start?

SUMMARY

Two important factors have to be established to ensure the successful development of your learning materials. The first is determining what tasks are needed to complete the job. The second is determining who can do those tasks and is available to do them. All of your planning will be for nothing if you have not identified the right tasks and assigned them to the people who can do the job.

The first chapter reviews the various questions you will have to ask yourself before you begin the development of your learning materials and suggests a method for formalizing your answers to those questions as part of your documentation.

INTRODUCTION

When you are assigned to the task of developing learning materials – don't panic! Wait and do that later!

This chapter is about sorting out what has to be done and who can help you do it. It is about not panicking but sitting down quietly with a pen and a couple of sheets of papers or at your computer, and making a list of each of the items that you will need to reflect upon and questions you will need to answer so you can start developing your course materials. Once you have completed your lists you will need to consider making your answers to the various questions part of your documentation by developing a series of task sheets.

ISSUES

Two of the major items you will be asked to consider in this chapter are time and budget. It is essential that you give attention to these items as they are very important to the success of your project. Chapter 3 will describe in greater detail the issue of time and Chapter 8 will review the budget as part of the evaluative criteria of your learning materials. However, wouldn't it be great if you had a better idea of what your learning materials project might need in both time and money before you got to those chapters?

SORTING THINGS OUT

The assumption is made here that you have some idea of the extent of the learning materials you are going to have to develop. Many details still have to be worked out, but overall you are in control and ready to take on the first phase of the project.

This phase of developing learning materials will require you to understand that materials development takes place in four distinct stages. These stages are:

● *Gathering information:* the process of gathering information to help you determine the focus, priorities and guidelines for your learning materials.
● *Materials development:* where you determine the details of your learning material, including the aims and objectives, their sequence and the delivery strategies.
● *Evaluation:* where you determine the process and procedure for evaluating the learners and the learning materials.
● *Materials production:* where your format and packaging decisions are finalized and the materials are produced.

As noted above, this first phase of the project is the part where you will need to write out, reflect upon and answer various questions for each of the above development stages. The questions and answers you come up with must, of course, be appropriate to the organization for which you work and the various constraints placed upon you by that organization.

Use the information gathering phase of the work as a way of determining the priorities and focus of the learning materials.

INFORMATION-GATHERING QUESTIONS YOU WILL NEED TO ASK YOURSELF

What is the topic for the materials?

You should be able to determine the answer to this question from the information you have been given to date. Remember that this should be a short, general description and may be subject to change.

How will the new materials fit with existing materials?

This question is a little more complex than the one above but you should be able to answer it based on discussions you should have held with the person who assigned you to the project. However, here you will need to go a couple of steps further and determine the total programme developed for the learner and where and how the materials you are developing will fit into that programme. The question is an important one as it will help you make some decisions regarding content and planning any pre- and co-requisites that might be required. It will also help you eliminate any repeating or overlapping of learning materials.

The key here is to remain flexible. Try not to cast things in stone – they will be subject to change.

What are the goals or aims of the materials?

To answer this question you will have to ensure that the goals determined for the materials (assuming that some have been set at this early stage) outline the general or overall outcomes that have been set for the course itself. Remember that these goals are the ones suggested for the course and are *not* your personal goals. Remember too that goals or aims can also include assumptions and values that are going to be conveyed in the materials. You will be determining course goals in much greater detail when you complete your Course Information Document (CID) – see Chapter 2.

Who is the audience for the materials?

This question is very important because the more you can describe your audience the more likely you are to develop relevant learning materials. Who are they? How old are they? What kind of experiences have they had? These questions can be asked of all members of the learning community, from the very young to the not so young, at all levels of education and training. If they are young adults or older you might want to find out if they work and, if so, what kind of work they do. Answers to these and other similar questions will help you determine the kind of learning materials you will have, want or need to produce.

It might be wise for you to consider putting together a simple questionnaire to find out more about the people who are going to be in your classroom. Ask them questions about their likes and dislikes in terms of learning materials. For example, ask them what their favourite subject was in school and why it was a favourite. (What you are trying to find out here is what teaching style and or materials they liked best.) Remember that adults make choices and if they make the decision to come to your course, they will want to learn something and they will want their money's worth. Of course young people also want their money's worth but they have less choice about being in your classroom. Ask your potential audience what they *need* to learn and what they *need* to get from the materials you are planning.

Try to keep your questionnaire to one page and make sure you keep the questions simple. Use a scale such as Likert (see Further Reading (Ebel and Sax)) or some form of rating system to quantify reaction. Remember that Likert scales usually employ a number of choices that express different degrees of agreement or disagreement and yield ordinal measurements. If you prefer using open-ended questions, you will find that you get the best results from asking your questions in an interview situation and structuring the interview around a questionnaire like that shown in Figure 1.1.

If you keep your questionnaire to one page, people are more likely to fill it out.

What constraints, such as time, financial and human, am I facing?

This question will require you to consider each of the following:

- How much time do I have to do the job?
- How much money is being allocated to the project?
- Who can I get to help me do the job?
- How long can I have the help for?

These are four problems in particular relating to the systematic development of course materials. The first is convincing those who assigned you the task that it can't be done in a couple of weeks. Second is convincing people that you may need money up-front to pay for the preparation (writing, printing and the like) of the materials. Third is convincing people that you are going to need to do the job, and fourth

Questions	Probing
What do you hope to get out of the course that you are signed up for?	Find out if expectations are realistic.
What will have to take place during the course to have it meet your expectations?	Do you see any problems with your expectations?
What do you want to learn during the course?	Is what you hope to learn going to be useful for a job you hope to do? In what way will it be useful?
What do you hope to do differently when you have completed the course?	Ask for specific examples; try to connect to what you know about the course to date.
Is there anything else?	
Specific questions can be asked about particular aspects of the course you have to develop materials for; ask about aspects of the materials that might be new to the learner or that you are considering trying for the first time.	
Is there anything else that we have not talked about that you think is important for me to know?	

Figure 1.1   *Interview questionnaire (adapted with permission from Earl, T (1987)* The Art and Craft of Course Design)

When making your time calculations, consider there to be only 28 hours in a week – the rest of the time will be taken up doing other things.

is convincing others that those who make up the materials development team may need time away from their regular duties and/or some form of compensation for the extra hours they are going to put in.

When you are developing learning materials in an education or any other setting for that matter, there are a number of fairly consistent rules of thumb that you can use to determine the time needed for the actual development of your various learning materials. The first rule states that you will need approximately 20 hours of development time (this includes gathering information, materials development, the design of an evaluation scheme and the production of the materials) for every one hour of course time if you use print-based materials and they are delivered directly to the learners in a face-to-face mode.

The kind of materials you are developing, however, will change the way you use the 20:1 formula. If you are developing materials for an intensive two- or three-day seminar or workshop (12 to 18 hours of course time) for example, you will find the 20:1 formula fairly consistent. However, if you are developing typical semester-long materials of 30, 45 or 60 hours in length, the 20:1 formula will not work quite as well, as the learners will not be spending all of those hours interacting with the learning materials. In this case you will have to try to estimate the time the learners will be spending with the materials and make your calculations accordingly.

For those of you not working in a training situation or who think that you don't develop materials for short courses, remember that you often teach in short time blocks, only here the short time is not called a course: it now becomes a topic, a unit or a subject (part of a larger whole). Your development time in this situation is the time spent developing your support or resource materials (all of the other 'stuff' has been done for you by the 'curriculum specialists'). Typically you do not develop all of your material at the beginning but you stretch it out over the time you are delivering the materials. If you think that 200 or more hours of materials development time is unreasonable or does not apply to you, just think back to the many nights and weekends you spent sitting at your desk preparing lessons for the upcoming week(s).

If you are involved in the design and development of video materials, development time and actual product development time increases to 40 to 50 hours for every one hour of video material. However, development time increases even more substantially if you are involved in putting together computer-based learning materials such as CD ROM or video disk. Here the ratio can be as high as 300 or more hours of development time to one hour of course materials. You should remember, however, that educational video or a computer-based learning module should rarely extend beyond one hour, so a development time of 300 or more hours (three or four months of full-time work) is fairly usual and acceptable.

What kind of expertise will I need to get the job done?

When you answer this question you are going to have to rely on your personal network, your knowledge of the people in that network, their abilities, their commitment to a project, their availability, their expertise and their commitment to you. You are going to have to develop time lines with realistic milestones to keep them on target, templates to ensure they do what you need them to do, and you are going to have to help them do it. You will also have to be prepared to find someone else to do the job if things go wrong. Figure 1.2 outlines the kind of expertise you will need to call on to get various types of materials development projects completed.

Don't forget that you may want to use video materials as part of your CBL package. This means that you should add a script writer, camera person and a director to your CBL list.

Type of teaching/ learning materials to be developed	Expertise required
Print-based materials	<ul><li>Instructional designer</li><li>Subject-matter experts</li><li>Writer(s)</li><li>Editor</li><li>Graphic artist</li><li>Information input person</li><li>Desktop publisher</li><li>Project manager (if the project is a large one)</li></ul>
Computer-based learning materials	<ul><li>Instructional designer</li><li>Subject-matter experts</li><li>Writer(s)</li><li>Editor</li><li>Graphic artist</li><li>Computer programmer</li><li>Project manager (if the project is a large one)</li></ul>
Audio/visual-based learning materials	<ul><li>Instructional designer</li><li>Subject-matter experts</li><li>Writer(s)</li><li>Script writer</li><li>Director</li><li>Camera person</li><li>Editor</li><li>Project manager (if the project is a large one)</li></ul>

Figure 1.2   *Project expertise needed*

Remember that the development of computer- or video-based materials often needs print-based resource materials so you may have to call on expertise from more than one area. Remember too that, depending upon the size of the project, you may have to play multiple roles or persuade others to take on more than one task.

As you review Figure 1.2, it is important that you understand that for certain projects you may, because of their size, need project management help. Don't try to manage a large project by yourself.

Another point worth noting is that when you are involved in the production of audio/video materials you should try to engage the help of professional actors and/or presenters, rather than the subject-matter expert (SME) to work in front of the camera. In the end it will save you both time and money and you will realize a far superior product.

How much material has to be produced?

It's quite possible that when you were asked to develop the learning materials a time rather than an amount was specified, that possibly ranged from one day (six hours) to one semester or even longer. Being presented with a time for the length of your materials when you do not know what is going to be included, just adds another dimension to the challenge of learning materials development. A typical strategy at this stage is to note the time you have been given on the CID (see Chapter 2) in the field trial section and let it go, for now. Remember, however, that you have been given a very important and valuable piece of information that you will need when you start developing your time line.

Once you reach the profile stage and you have a fairly definitive idea of what and how much is going to be included as part of the materials so that they provide a viable learning experience, then you will determine how, and if, it will fit into the given time frame.

MATERIALS DEVELOPMENT QUESTIONS YOU WILL NEED TO ASK YOURSELF

What are the objectives of the materials?

As with the question regarding goals, you should be able to get the answer to this question from your CID. You will, however, need to ensure that the objectives written there are measurable and contain at a minimum a statement of performance that indicates how the learner will achieve the competences set out in the materials. Remember that objectives can help you determine:

- material content
- teaching methodologies
- types of learning materials
- types of learner evaluation
- evaluation procedures

Try to get a list of the topics to be delivered to the learners rather than just a time frame for presentation

If you find that you have too much material for the time available consider a number of pre- and postlearning activities.

Use the materials development phase of the work as a way to determine the course details and your delivery strategies.

Use the list given in Chapter 4 of this book as a basic guide when writing your performance objectives

At this stage the objectives, like your goals, can be fairly broad statements of intent and will be subject to scrutiny and possible change during the profile session. However, that does not mean they can be ignored. Use the following description of the characteristics of an objective proposed by Gronlund to review any objectives that have been written to date. An objective:

● is a statement about the learner *not* the teacher
● refers to the behaviour of the learner and specifies what he/she *needs to know*. It also defines knowing by indicating how learners are to demonstrate their knowledge
● is stated in terms of an *end performance* and so should be the description of that end performance rather than a method for reaching it.

What am I going to include in the materials?

This question is one that you will have to attend to with great care. The true answer you will only get from your profile session as it should list all the topics for which materials are to be developed. At this stage of the project you should have completed the content section of the CID and at least have some idea of what are going to be considered as possible topics. You are going to have to make sure that the topics that have been identified are those *needed* by the learner rather than those you or your SME think would be *nice* for the learner to learn. It would also be wise at this stage for you to check some of the other learning materials and make sure there is no overlap. This is, of course, related to the question asked earlier regarding how your materials will fit with existing materials.

How is the content to be sequenced?

Like the previous question you will only get the true answer once you have completed the profile and had it validated. For the moment however, you should review the list of topics to see if a sequence can be determined or arrange the topics so that those that depend on knowledge of a previous topic are closely positioned. Doing this will help you be well-prepared for the profile session. To help you arrange topics in this way you may want to consider developing one or more concept maps where the key topic is placed in the centre of a blank page and lines drawn from it to all of its related topics.

What instructional strategies should be used?

Here it is important for you to consider how your materials will be delivered to the learner. Many delivery options are open to you, ranging from the lecture to discussion and debate to simulation; however, there are some criteria that you may wish to consider as you review each of your delivery options. These are:

Try to keep your learning strategies as simple as possible. Your learners will appreciate it!

- If I use this strategy will my learners be learning at a simple knowledge level, an application level or a synthesis level? What is best for them?
- What is my familiarity with the strategy? If I'm not that familiar with it, how and where can I practise?
- What is my motivation to try something new?
- How much time do I really have to prepare these learning materials?
- What are the needs of my learners?
- How well do the learners know the delivery strategy I'm considering? Are they going to be confused?
- What constraints am I facing with regard to lesson time, group size and both the learning and physical environment?
- What role do I expect my learners to play and what role do they expect me to play?

What other resources will be needed?

It is important that you determine the resources you will need before you actually need them. Previously, you considered time, human and financial constraints. Now you need to consider a number of other things. For example, is the physical space in which you now work large enough; do you have enough furniture? Are the computers and computing power you have adequate for the job? Remember that even the most mundane of computer applications can take up large chunks of hard disk space and any sophisticated materials development work is going to need huge amounts of disk space. Do you have the facilities to make back-up copies of your work? Do you have access to reference materials and all the various consumable items you will need over the life of the project? Rough out a plan of what you need.

WHAT EVALUATION STRATEGIES SHOULD I USE?

As part of your learning materials development you will need to develop an assessment of one type or another to help you diagnose, prescribe, grade and evaluate the materials you are going to develop.

Use the evaluation phase of the work to help you evaluate the learning materials, the delivery strategy and the learning that has taken place.

Diagnosis provides information about your learners' remediation needs. Prescriptive decisions are very much like diagnostic decisions, except that they take place during the course rather than before it. Grading follows the course and tells you what your learners have or have not learned. The evaluation should provide you with conclusions that you can use to determine if the learners have learned anything new, are able to apply that new material in an everyday situation and if your method of communication was effective.

When considering the various evaluation strategies you are going to use, ask yourself each of the following questions.

Did the learners achieve the goals and objectives set out in the materials?

As part of the development process you are going to have to develop a methodology to answer this evaluation question.

Are the materials being delivered in an effective and cost-effective manner?

Developing a methodology to answer this evaluation question will entail your taking into consideration all of the internal and external constraints that impact your materials, and making comparisons with other materials. These might include the cost and type of materials, the venue, the time of the day, month or year the materials were delivered and the type of learner. All of these issues will have to be examined to ensure that a basis for sound decision making about retaining and subsequent delivery of the materials has been developed.

How can the materials be improved?

Material improvement is based on a sound summative evaluation procedure that is going to have to be designed prior to the materials being delivered the first time. As part of this procedure a pilot study or field trial could be considered.

Are the learners happy with the materials?

This question is not meant to imply that the evaluation carried out should be a 'happiness index' which simply asks the participants how they liked the materials. Typically this type of index only measures the 'entertrainment' (sic) value of a course and the results are sometimes difficult to apply to all learners, because the suggestions are often self-cancelling.

It is important then that you design something more than a happiness index. To do this you will have to determine what you need to evaluate and design the questions so they assist the learner to supply you with the right information.

MATERIALS PRODUCTION QUESTIONS YOU WILL NEED TO ASK YOURSELF

What kind of learning materials are appropriate for the learners?

Use the materials production phase of the work to help you finalize the material format as well as produce the materials.

It is important that you plan how your learning materials are to be written. If, for example, you are going to have one or more writers helping you develop materials, it is imperative that you know exactly what you want from them and how you want the materials formatted. You will have to make decisions regarding what access devices are going to be included in your materials, such as contents page, introductions, headings and summaries. You will also have to make decisions regarding illustrations, photographs and graphs and how these might be incorporated into the materials.

How should the learning materials be formatted?

Keep your materials format as simple as possible, that way para professional help can be used when revisions are needed.

Here you will be required to make a number of decisions regarding text formatting, physical page layout, the use of columns on the page, font type and size, the numbering system you intend to use and if you are going to print on both sides of the page. Remember that your formatting decisions will have to be made in the context of the maturity level of your learners and the topic of the materials.

What should be the readability level of my materials?

Readability is all of those elements in printed learning materials that affect the ability of the learner to understand them, learn from them, read them at optimum speed and that make them interesting. There are a number of different readability indices available to you, such as the Gunning Fox Index, Flesch-Kincaid index and the Lensear Formula. As part of the development of your learning materials a readability index will need to be applied to ensure the materials are being developed to the correct level for your audience.

How are the learning materials to be packaged?

The packaging of learning materials is important in terms of overall cost, learner ability to interact with the materials and learner motivation. For example, if your materials are going to be placed in a two- or three-ring binder and you have 100 or more learners, then costs could be high. As an alternative you might want to consider the use of a simple plastic cover, some form of spiral binding, or staple and glue. You may also wish to consider packaging the materials yourself or, if you work in a large educational organization, having your materials preparation centre or in-house print shop do the job.

Remember to consider your page margins as they have to be wide enough to accept the kind of packaging you want for your materials.

As you consider packaging also consider your learners and how they are going to physically access and interact with your materials. For example, if you are using print materials and you have made the decision to leave enough white space on the page for learner notes, then it would be helpful if the materials package opened flat. Remember your own difficulties in trying to balance a book on one of those small writing tables attached to the arm rests in a lecture theatre or trying to take notes in the margin of a book that did not lie flat.

Finally, consider the length and size of your print materials. If they are going to be many pages in length, should they be packaged all together or should they be broken into two or more smaller parts? Will having the materials bound together make the package too heavy or awkward for the learner to carry? Consider how the motivation level of the learner might be affected by receiving a package of materials that is five or six centimetres thick! But also consider the additional packaging costs if materials are broken into smaller parts and the possible problems of ensuring that the learner brings the right materials to be right class. What you will have to do is find an acceptable balance between the various extremes. If your packaging considerations include computer-based materials you must give thought to the format – disk or CD ROM – the applications used, the hardware needed to run the program and the ability of the learner to retrieve the information.

What other materials will be needed to enhance the package with respect to learning?

Assuming that you have given due consideration to the question of instructional strategies posed under materials development, and made some decisions about delivery options, this question asks you to go one step further and reflect on what other things you might need to enhance that delivery, or help you deliver the learning materials to the learners. These might simply be more print-based materials or could include slides, video or computer-based materials of various types. Whatever they are, you can use the same criteria that you used for determining your instructional strategies to help you in your selection.

What am I going to do about copyright?

A great many of the materials that you will want to use will have some form of copyright attached to them. You are going to have to deal with this for a large project by having, as part of your development team, one person responsible for checking copyright. You will have to set up for all team members a means of keeping track of the materials being used and their source, as well as a system for your organization to make the necessary payments to the various copyright holders.

Certain materials such as cartoons, comic strips and video clips of sports events command high user fees and you will need to be aware of those fees and the value of using such materials compared to developing your own or, with a slight modification in your plans and with no serious loss in the learning quality of the materials, not using them at all.

Remember that almost everything created privately and originally after 1 April 1989 is copyrighted and its use is restricted.

What are the costs?

A number of the questions posed so far ask you to consider things that could have high cost implications. You should now go back over each of your answers to those questions and determine how you can work out the cost for each of the decisions you have made. For example, if you have determined that your materials are to be formatted in a particular way, will you have to hire someone to do it or can it be done by a member of your team? If you have made certain decisions regarding packaging, can those decisions be supported with sufficient funds? If you have decided to develop other support materials, have you got the expertise to do it or do you have to go elsewhere at a higher cost? Given the length of the project, has your team got sufficient release time or will you be left high and dry two months from the end? Consider what kind of general costs you are facing with respect to copyright.

Some of these costs are, of course, impossible to determine at this stage. But you need to be prepared. At the risk of sounding overly pessimistic you should consider a worst-case scenario, set out a budget plan and try to ensure that you have all the various contingencies covered.

It's time to work out the costs of the learning materials development project you have been assigned and present those findings to those who gave you the task. This is a critical stage in the life of any project and one that must be faced sooner rather than later.

MAKING YOUR THOUGHTS PART OF THE COURSE DOCUMENTATION

Once you have completed the preceding tasks you should consider finalizing your thoughts and making them part of your documentation. To help you do this you may wish to adapt the example of a typical task overview sheet shown in Figure 1.3 to suit your needs.

Stage 1: Gathering course information	
Item or question:	Course audience
Discussion:	Mid-teens of both sexes. Just entered the college system and could lack study skills needed for an independent study mobile. Questionnaire needed to gather more information
Resources needed:	Materials developer
Responsibility for action:	Materials developer
Time considerations:	Questionnaire development and administration
Budget considerations:	Directly attributable to the time plus required materials and photocopying
Product or outcome:	Questionnaire
Other:	N/A

Figure 1.3   *Task overview sheet*

CONCLUSION

This chapter has described a process to help you determine where to start a learning materials development project. It's important that you understand that quietly sitting and reflecting on the various questions suggested here will help you focus on the task at hand and help get the project off to a good start. Take the time to go through this process as soon as possible after you have been assigned to the project, as it will save you many hundreds of hours later on. Use the answers to the questions as part of your planning process and develop as much documentation as you can to help you be a more informed decision maker.

Chapter 2
How Do I Determine What I Really Need?

SUMMARY

A Course Information Document (CID) is designed to assist you gather information to help ensure that the important details about those materials you are to develop are well documented and the profile of what the learner has to achieve is correctly focused.

The CID is designed so that it can be used by anyone given the job of putting together learning materials. The form can be used in two different ways: it can be used to record the information you would gather during an interview with a subject-matter expert (SME) or it can be completed by you if you are the SME. In either case, the information must be verified by others involved in the materials development process.

This chapter will describe a method of information-gathering and provide an example of a pro-forma document that will help you gather all the information you will need to build a solid foundation of documentation.

INTRODUCTION

Gathering information prior to the development of your learning materials – the very idea can strike dread deep into your heart when you are asked to design, develop or modify learning materials. Gathering together all the information and documentation you will need conjures up thoughts of extensive research, surveys, questionnaires, endless data, reports and meetings and spending massive amounts of time.

The need to spend any amount of time at all in this area is often questioned by those waiting for the materials, and sometimes a tight deadline suggests that this phase be dropped or at least be as short as possible. However, getting the right information ready for the development of appropriate learning materials is an important task that must be systematically carried out if the materials are to provide a viable learning experience.

BACKGROUND

You have been given the job of 'Developing learning materials for ...' by some impossible date, with no significant amount of money at your disposal, and you need specific answers to questions like, 'What do I do now?' and, 'How can I find out what the learner needs to know?'

There is an extensive literature on the topic of gathering learning materials information and documentation (see the additional reading section at the end of this book). The problem for many potential learning material developers lies in the usefulness of the particular method being suggested in light of the information needed.

PRO-FORMA DOCUMENTATION

Pro-forma documents such as the CID suggested here can be used in a number of different and important ways, such as:

● serving as a memory aid during the development of your learning materials
● providing the basis for updates and any redevelopment of your learning materials in the future
● providing a consistent development methodology for different kinds of learning materials
● providing a sound basis for learning material development planning, including development time, human resource needs and costing
● providing a basis for the preparation of a budget.

The pro-forma documents described in this book are a CID, a one-page profile sheet (see Chapter 4) and a sub-profile sheet (see Chapter 5). Together they make up the data-gathering tools you will need to successfully collect all the information needed to design and develop your learning materials as well as support the actions you will be taking as you develop those materials. The forms will assist you in gathering the information you need for documentation and subsequent validation of the learning materials. Validation is important as it allows others to review what has been written and comment on its authenticity and accuracy. The aim of the CID is to assist you to gather course data quickly and ensure the course profile is correctly focused and that other important course details are well-documented. The profile sheet outlines all the skills and competences the learner must learn as part of the course for which you are developing the learning materials. The sub-profile sheet fills in the essential details of the learning materials that are not provided for on the profile sheet.

COURSE INFORMATION DOCUMENT (CID)

Use the course information documentation as the basis for your course materials documentation file.

The CID described here is designed so that it can be used by anyone given the task of putting together learning materials. It is important that you understand that the various questions discussed in this chapter as part of the information-gathering process can be placed in any format appropriate to your needs or the needs of the team developing the learning materials. An example of a typical CID is shown at the end of this chapter. Take a look at it now, before you read the rest of the chapter.

The form can be used in two different ways: you can use it to record the information that you gather during an interview with an SME or, if you are the SME, you can complete it yourself. In either case the information gathered must be verified by others involved in the project.

Basic information

The first questions you have to ask are straightforward: 'What is the working title of the course?' and, 'Who are the subject-matter experts who are going to help me complete the task of developing learning materials?' It is important to remember that there are many 'experts' and you will be faced with trying to balance the various tasks that need to be completed and ensuring that all those involved are working on the task(s) most appropriate for them. These tasks can include providing information for the development of both the CID and the profile, validating the profile, developing the actual learning materials, validating those materials and/or developing ancillary materials. It is in your best interest as the materials developer to make sure that the people listed on the CID are the most appropriate ones for that part of the development process.

The audience

The second set of questions deal with the audience – those people you are developing the materials for; the people who are often ignored in the rush to get the materials ready. As you consider who the course is really for, the answer you come up with may significantly alter the direction and content of the materials you end up producing. You may also wish to consider a secondary audience, as the possibility of a wider audience may help increase the potential for funding and marketing.

As you are reviewing the audience for your materials you should consider a number of factors such as their:

- age
- educational level
- reading level
- motivation for learning
- cultural background
- previous experiences
- abilities
- attitudes.

The purpose

The purpose section of the CID asks three questions. The first, 'Why is the course being developed?', provides the rationale for the work you are doing. The determination of a rationale will be one of the most difficult questions the person you are interviewing, or you, will have to answer. Whether you are completing the CID in an interview situation or completing it yourself, you will have to allow time for the rationale to be formulated. In an interview situation you may need to work with your SME for a significant amount of time, helping them articulate and subsequently put the rationale in writing. When the rationale is completed it will help you in writing goals and objectives and help focus the development of the profile.

You may find that the rationale will have to be a compromise worked out between what is needed by the learners and others involved in the materials development project. Whatever the outcome, discussion will have taken place, opinions will have been aired and positions taken. For many materials development projects this is a healthy process and will help you be better prepared for potential problems.

The outcomes

The outcome portion of the CID deals with goals and objectives. Here you will be required to determine the various goals for the materials you are developing and what the learner must do in order to achieve these goals through the development of a series of objectives.

The writing of goals and objectives suggests measurement of some kind. However, trying to measure something that is not clearly defined is very difficult and it will be hard for you to know what materials should be developed unless a clear picture of the end result has been determined. As a developer of learning materials you will require a fairly precise set of goals and objectives for your own guidance as well as to determine what has to be achieved by the learner.

Useful goals and objectives will help you answer the following questions:

- What should learners be able to do with the skills and knowledge they have learned?
- Under what conditions should learners be able to do the tasks that they have learned?
- How well must it be done? What are the standards or competences that the learners must achieve?

A meaningful goal or objective is one that:

- communicates its intent by excluding the greatest number of possible meanings other than those that you intended.

Objectives are useful in the design of instructional materials as they tell you where you are going, how you are going to get there, and how you will know when you have arrived. A useful objective is one that allows you to make the largest number of decisions relevant to its achievement and measurement.

The evaluation

The evaluation portion of the CID focuses on how you will measure the course goals and objectives. Typically you develop assessments of one type or another to diagnose, prescribe, grade and evaluate instruction along with the actual learning materials (see Chapter 1).

Diagnosis provides information about your learners' needs. Prescriptive decisions are very much like diagnostic decisions, except that they take place during the course rather than before it. Grading will follow your instruction and should tell you what the learners have or have not learned. It should also provide you with conclusions that you can use to determine if they have learned anything new, are able to apply that new material in an everyday situation and if your method of communication was effective.

It is important that your materials are designed to be focused on the learner *not* the teacher.

The content/treatment

In the content section of the CID you will have to develop a list of the various topics being considered as part of the course. This list is important as it will help you better focus your profile session and better determine what learning materials will have to be developed. Whether you are completing the CID during an interview with an SME or completing it yourself, you will need to ensure that the list is based on the needs of the particular job or life skill the learner *needs* to learn, *not* on materials that would be *nice* for the learner to know.

It is important that in this section you outline just the main 'need to know' topics as they are understood at the time of writing. Try not to get bogged down in details. You also should not be too concerned that what you are writing is the last word on the matter. The next phase of the process is the development of the profile based on the course goals and objectives and these, along with the list of content topics, will determine the actual 'need to know' content of the learning materials. Your CID can be updated later.

As part of the content section you will also have to consider how you are going to deliver or present the materials to the learner. Here it is important that you ensure that the focus is on the learners and their learning needs.

As you complete the treatment portion of the document you should consider an alternative range of delivery methods. These methods should be within the resources of the institution, yourself or the teacher who will deliver the materials, and most important, the learner. Typical treatments can include a combination of some or all of the following delivery methodologies:

Case study   Demonstration
Discussion or debate   Drill and practice

Laboratories   Role play
Simulation   Field trip(s)

The field trial

One area much neglected in the development of learning materials is the field trial. Time and budget constraints are the reasons most often given for not conducting one. Factors such as the materials being a 'once only' delivery event and the notion that materials can be fixed as delivery takes place so the next group of learners can benefit from the revisions, also contribute to neglect in this area.

As part of the field trial, three important questions need to be asked. The first, 'How are the materials to be presented?' raises issues about the size of the learning group and the physical layout of the area best suited for the delivery of the materials. Many constraints will be placed on you here and some compromise will have to be made between the ideal and what is available. For example, you have determined that small group discussion is the best method to help the learners develop themselves; however, all that is available is a large lecture theatre. Can you hold small group discussions in a lecture theatre? The answer of course, is yes, but it will take more planning and good organizational skills on the part of the person delivering that portion of the materials.

As the designer, at this stage of the development process, your role is to note the ideal but have a number of contingencies at your fingertips ready to put into place as the ideal slips away. Try to make these decisions against your background knowledge of the facility being used to deliver the materials and how the environment might affect the delivery of the materials and the learning that needs to take place. You may also wish to consider using some form of course support document to describe the infrastructure needed to support a typical course offering. This document could be made part of your course documentation package. (See Book 2 Chapter 3 in this series.)

The second question refers to the estimated date by which learning materials are to be completed. You should ensure this estimate is as accurate as possible by developing a viable product schedule (see Chapter 3).

The third and final question regarding the field trial concerns scheduling. When you are reviewing scheduling consider the concept of Just-In-Time (JIT) learning where the opportunity for the learner to gain knowledge of a particular topic is offered just prior to that knowledge being needed. For example, if a course has been designed to train administrators to develop a budget and present it for review prior to the start of the financial year, then you may wish to consider offering the course to coincide with those events.

Other

The final section of the CID deals with reviewing any existing materials available to support the new materials you are developing. Completing this review will help others overcome the perception that you as the materials developer are 'reinventing the wheel' and help reduce any duplication.

You can attach a list of support materials to the CID and add to it as needed. It is also important that you carry out a review of similar topic materials to determine how suitable they might be for use with current materials.

Finally, remember that you may need to obtain copyright permission for the materials being prepared for inclusion or adaptation in your learning materials.

FINALIZING THE CID

If you completed the CID during an interview with an SME you will need to write it up, ensuring that the goal(s) and objective statements are measurable entities and appropriate for your use as you develop the learning materials. Once you have the form written-up you should return it to the SME for validation. The information in the document should also be validated by an outside group of the SME's peers. If you completed the form yourself it can go straight to an outside group of your choice for validation. The validation can be a simple affair with each member of the validation team making suggestions as to the required changes, or it can undergo a more rigorous treatment using a Delphi technique.

The Delphi method involves sending the CID out to all members of a validation team for review. As each CID is returned, a new version is developed according to that person's viewpoint and consolidated into the other copies of the CID as needed. Once this has been completed for all the members of the validation group, the new CID is sent to each member of the group for comment and review. As each review is completed the returned copies are again consolidated into one new CID and again sent out to the validation group. This review process continues until only one version of the CID remains. This remaining

Like many things in the business of course development, the Course Information Document will be subject to a number of changes, so keep it as flexible as possible.

CID is now considered validated and ready to be used as the basis for the course documentation. You will need to place the final version of the CID into the course documentation file ready for use both prior to and during the profiling session.

CONCLUSION

In this chapter the discussion has centred around the development of a Course Information Document. The questions you have to ask, either yourself if you are completing the form, or an SME if you are interviewing someone, are designed to help you better determine the scope of the project in which are you involved. The CID, when completed, will form the basis for carrying out the profile session and help you better determine the techniques you will have to employ to deliver the learning materials to the learners. The form is an important addition to the documentation you will need to complete the project. It will provide the basis for the many decisions you and others will be making regarding the allocation of both human and financial resources and the overall development of the learning materials.

Following is a completed example of a CID. The format used here is just one of many appropriate for gathering the kind of information you need at this early stage of the project, and in that sense the format as such is not important. What is important are the questions you ask and how you use the answers to those questions to help you through the next stages of the project.

Course Information Document

Course Working Title:

The Preparation and Presentation of Assessment Appeals

Subject Matter Experts:

Profile Group
J. George, D. Formane, M. Stone
D. Jones, D. Malone, J. Moloney
R. James, G. Wong, A. McLean, F. Wilson

Course SMEs
J. George, G. Wong

Law advisers
L. Birch, B. Graham

Recommended Teachers
J. George, G. Wong

Audience

Principal Audience (Who):

What group of learners will benefit from the course?

Practising assessors and tax agents.

Secondary Audience:

Will any other group of learners benefit from the course?

Municipal administrators and local tax agents.

Purpose

Rationale (Why):

Why is there a need to produce this course?

All assessments are subject to ratepayer review and complaint on an annual basis. The assessor must be prepared to defend all of his/her assessments before the Assessment Appeal Board as the equity of an assessment may be affected because of their presentation to the tribunal.

Outcomes: Goals

Learner Goals:

What areas of learning, understanding or appreciation will the learners get from this course?

Upon completion of this course the learner should be able to:

Present information to the Assessment Appeal Board tribunal in a concise and comprehensive manner and remain impartial within the scope of the relevant legislation.

Outcomes: Objectives

Learner Objectives:

What must the learners do to achieve the objectives?

Upon completion of this course the learner should be able to:

define the legislative authority of the Board
describe the hearing procedures
prepare effective presentation materials
present an effective written case
present an effective oral case
advocate the assessment position.

Evaluation

Evaluation:

How will the learner achieve the course goals and objectives?

What form of content testing is most appropriate?

Successful completion of the course goals indicates that the learner is able to:
present an effective written case to the Board
present an effective oral case to the Board.

As part of the evaluation strategy, a reaction evaluation will determine the effectiveness of the course materials.

Content

Scope:

List the content topics to be covered and note the depth of coverage or emphasis.

The course should include but not be limited to:

Pre-hearing preparation

Presentation skills at the hearing

Post-hearing requirements

Dealing with the tax agent

When to get additional expertise

When to involve the Council/Municipal Secretary

Reacting to evidence from the appellant

Adjournments and postponements

Written reasons regarding the presentation of the case (facts vs argument)

What facts are pertinent to the case.

Treatment:

How is the content of this course to be presented to the learner? Identify your delivery method, instructional materials and application of media.

Workshop format with case studies and role plays to determine presentation skills.

Field Trial

Use:

How is the course to be presented? Indicate class size and room arrangements. Attach separate diagram(s) as necessary.

Standard classroom. Class size 20 learners. See attached room arrangement diagram.

Time:

Completion date of learning materials.

August 15, next year.

Course Scheduling:

Indicate the best time of year/time of day for presentation of the course.

Courses can be presented at any time.

Other

Support Materials:

Indicate the support materials that will be needed.

See attached list.

Existing Materials:

Indicate the existing materials that may be required to complete the learning materials. Attach additional sheets as required.

Reviewing the courses 'Understanding the Municipal Taxation Act' and 'Assessing Multi-residential improvements' for material appropriate for this course. Take a case to a mock Appeal Board. Discuss content with developer of above courses and SMEs at the Legal Resource Centre.

Chapter 3
Making It All Run Smoothly

SUMMARY

Developing learning materials is a task that requires systematic planning to ensure that they are delivered on time to the learners. It is essential that those guiding the development of learning materials understand the fundamentals of task analysis enough to be able to break down the four areas of course development into their various components and assign each of those components a realistic time line so the job can be completed within the given time frame.

This chapter will review the concept of working backwards to establish a viable time line and describe how a typical learning materials project can be broken into sub-systems and how those sub-systems are linked together to enable you to get an overall picture of the project.

INTRODUCTION

This chapter is about keeping your learning materials project on time. It will use, as an example, the design and development of print-based learning materials that include both teacher and learner workbooks, teaching aids, learner support and evaluation materials. The chapter will discuss each of the following:

- What tasks do I have to do?
- What order should I do them in?
- When do I have to start each task so I can get the materials ready on time?

You should note that the example used at the end of the chapter contains most of the tasks associated with a typical learning materials development project. No attempt has been made to describe the details of project management such as logic tables, slack time, PERT, Gantt charts and the like. For that the reader should consult the many texts on the matter, starting with those listed in the further reading section at the end of the book.

WHAT TASKS DO I HAVE TO DO?

Perhaps the best thing that you can wish for when you are assigned to a materials development project is that you are given the approximate date when the materials are needed. You may recall those words that set your heart aflutter: '... yes, I want a three-day course and it has to be ready for next term' or, 'You have been assigned to teach such and such next term'. You might not think so at the time but you have been given a very valuable piece of information: when the materials are needed. It is from this snippet of information that you can determine when the materials must actually be ready and start to plan how to get them to the learners. If you are not given an approximate completion date you must make sure that you get one as soon as possible because, without it, it will be very difficult to get the project organized.

In order to get started you will have to think backward from your completion date so you can:

● Plan all of the tasks you will have to complete.
● Determine what tasks you will have to do before other tasks.
● Determine the timing for each task and the total project.

Unlike some other projects you might have been involved in where you have to start from scratch, the design and development of learning materials has, for the most part, already been broken down into four sub-systems that contain a fairly standard set of tasks that have to be performed. As you become more experienced at developing learning materials you will learn to juggle many of these tasks depending on the circumstances you face at that time.

The first task you will have to do is to review your various sub-systems. As noted above, each sub-system for learning materials development has been previously determined for you (see Chapter 1). These are:

- Gathering information
- Materials development
- Evaluation
- Materials production.

Your next task is to determine all of the various sub-systems tasks that have to be carried out. This is similar to that which you did in Chapter 1, except that here you will have to consider actual tasks rather than thinking in generalities. Typical tasks that fall into each of the sub-systems are shown in Figure 3.1.

Once you have determined each of the various tasks that you will have to complete, your next job will be to list each of the sub-tasks that need to be done. These sub-tasks will change, of course, depending upon the exact nature of the work you are doing. Typical sub-tasks for just one of the tasks in each of the sub-systems might be as shown in Figure 3.2.

WHAT ORDER SHOULD I DO THEM IN?

Once you have compiled your sub-task list you should number each task in the order in which it will have to be done. It's possible that when you were writing your list, you unconsciously put them in some kind of order. If you did, great; if not, spend some time ordering them. The list that you produce will, of course, be linear in nature but there will be certain tasks that can be carried out simultaneously. For example, as the profile is being validated the initial course treatment can be developed. Or the learner workbook can be started, using the sub-profile as a guide, before the course treatment is finalized. Go back through your list and determine which tasks can be completed at the same time. A word here about treatment: treatment refers to the methodology or strategy used to deliver the learning materials. Typical delivery strategies are described in Chapter 6 of this book.

HOW MUCH TIME DO I HAVE?

After having put all of the tasks in order, your next job is to start with your end date and work backward through each task in turn and determine the time each will require. The problem is that developing learning materials is not an exact science and so every materials development project will be different. In most cases there are no set

Sub-system	Task
Gathering information	– Review and revise the Course Information Document – Develop the learner profile – Validate the profile – Revise the profile where needed – Develop the sub-profile – *Validate the learner profile** – Revise the sub-profile where needed
Materials Development	– *Develop learning material treatments** – Validate treatments – Revise treatments where needed
Evaluation	– Conduct field trial – Review and revise all field trial materials where needed – *First delivery of the materials** – Review and revise all learning materials where needed – Produce final learning materials master
Materials Production	– *Draft teacher workbook** – Validate teacher workbook – Revise teacher workbook where needed – Develop teaching aids – Review and revise teaching aids – Draft learner workbook – Validate learner workbook – Revise learner workbook where needed – Draft learner support materials – Review and revise learner support materials – Draft evaluation materials – Validate evaluation materials – Editor's final review – Produce field trial master

Figure 3.1   *Typical learning materials development tasks*
*Itemized in Figure 3.2

formulae to help you determine how much time a task such as drafting the teacher workbook will take; only from experience can you make such estimates. But before you have that experience you are going to have to determine answers to questions like, how long will the validation of a profile take or what is an acceptable length of time to allow a person to write a learner workbook?

Sub-system	Sub-task
Gathering Information	● *Validate the learner profile* – Set completion deadline – Develop profile template – Select validation group – Prepare instructions for the validation group – Send out profile to validation group – Telephone follow-up – Collect all revisions from profile group – Develop revised profile – Send profile out for final confirmation
Materials Development	● *Develop learning material treatments* – Review profile – Review criteria for the selection of instructional strategies – Select appropriate treatment(s)
Evaluation	● *First delivery of the materials* – Set guidelines for teacher preparation – Prepare learning materials – Prepare teacher materials – Review teacher preparation – Ensure rooms are suitable – Book room(s) – Ensure all support materials and teaching aids are available
Materials Production	● *Draft teacher workbook* – Develop page format – Develop page format template – Determine guidelines for chapter objectives – Determine guidelines for chapter introduction, summary and other access devises – Determine guidelines for tables, graphs, charts, tables and illustrations – Determine guidelines for the evaluation of other resources – Determine text guidelines – Determine guidelines for readability testing

Figure 3.2   *Typical learning material development sub-tasks*

Your first source of help in answering these questions might be your colleagues and/or others that have benefited from having completed a similar project or projects. Your second source is simply the time you have available to you. You know that the project has to be completed by a certain date. You have your end date fixed, you know that it takes about 20 hours to develop one hour of print-based materials (see Chapter 1), so if your topic, subject, unit or module is 18 hours in length you have a total of 360 hours (18×20) to get all the task completed. A similar basic calculation can be carried out for any other kind of material you are developing. An indication of what 18 hours might translate into and when the learning materials will have to be planned and prepared, is given in Figure 3.3.

A typical course of 12 to 14 hours' duration takes about one month of actual materials development time. This includes developing both teacher and learner guides and other materials.

Course	Typical course duration	Documentation	Planning	Preparation
Training	Three days at six hours each	Up front By developer	All up front	All up front
School	Two hours per week for nine weeks	Up front By others	Some up front Some later	Some up front Most as needed
College/ University	One lecture and two tutorials per week for six weeks	Up front Can be by developer or others	Some up front Some later	Some up front Most as needed

Figure 3.3 *A typical 18-hour course translated for different areas of education*

Using this information, you can now determine how much time to assign to each of your sub-systems, then divide that time up among each of the various tasks. Once you have determined a time for each task you will need to add to that time all of the reasonable sources of delay that you can expect, such as scheduling problems (trying to get people together for profiling sessions or allowing busy people time to validate materials, for example) and any necessary revisions, and from this determine the time you will need. Typically most learning materials development projects stop at the review stage after the field trial, if there is a field trial at all, and rarely is the first time the materials are delivered included as part of the time available.

You will notice in the following example that the two dates have been placed next to each task box. The top date is the earliest date that

Don't confuse a revision with editing. Revision has to do with writing 2,000 words to finish up with 1,500. Editing has to do with checking and improving those words for clarity.

the task should start and the bottom date is the latest date the task can start if the project is to be finished on time.

A simple mathematical calculation suggested by Kliem and Ludin (1993) to help you determine your early and late start dates is:

Early start date – Early finish date *minus* duration of the task *plus* 1 day
Late start date – Late finish date *minus* duration of the task *plus* 1 day.

SAMPLE MATERIALS DEVELOPMENT PROJECT

The following is an example of how a typical learning materials project can be set out ready for you to discuss with those who assigned you the task and from whom you have to acquire the needed resources.

It is important that you understand that when you are engaged in the development of learning materials, each phase has outcomes in the form of products. As part of your job in making sure that the project stays on track and on budget you will have to determine exactly what these products are for each major part or sub-system of the project, and set up milestones with dates by which those products must be completed. These dates can be the same as the dates you have already determined for the project or they can be other dates based on different needs of the project. For example, even if a project time line, like the one above, has been calculated at 360 hours, the actual duration of the project might be spread out over a greater period of time. This could mean therefore that the product need not be actually delivered on the date specified on the network diagram.

So far the evaluation phase of the project has been treated as sandwiched between materials development and materials production. However, this is a somewhat artificial placement and should only be considered for planning purposes. As the actual time lines for the project are set out, the evaluation phase must move to its correct place, that is, after the field trial has been completed. This example reflects that change.

The following details about the sample learning materials project are important to your understanding of the remainder of the chapter:

● The materials being developed are for use in an intensive three-day (18 hours) workshop/seminar.

- One instructional designer has been assigned to develop the materials needed for the assessment, development and evaluation phases of the project. In addition, two writers and an editor have been assigned to the development of the materials needed for the production phase of the project.
- A total time of 28 hours per week has been allotted to the project, 28 hours being 75 per cent of a typical 37.5 hour week. This has resulted in a total of 12.8 (13) weeks being allotted for the actual length of the project.
- The total time determined for the project is approximately 360 hours (20×18 hours).
- The estimated time is approximately five days (28 hours) over the original estimate! (Hey, it happens to the best of us!)
- The project will start January 1 and end May 8 after the review of the evaluation from the field trial.
- The dates have been written using the convention month/day/year.

Gathering information

The first part of the network diagram (see Figure 3.4) shows all the various tasks that should be completed during the information-gathering phase of the project. This phase takes approximately 40 hours.

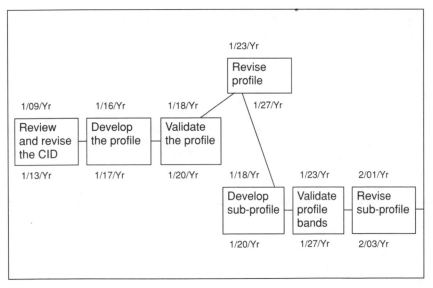

Figure 3.4 *Information-gathering tasks*

To ensure that this and the other phases of the project run smoothly you might wish to consider setting up an outcomes chart similar to that shown in Figure 3.5.

Gathering Information

Required resources
- Profile team
- Profile validation team
- Sub-profile team
- Sub-profile validation team

Product milestones
- Course Information Document   1/13/Yr
- Course Profile   1/27/Yr
- Course Sub-profile   2/03/Yr

Figure 3.5   *Products of the information-gathering phase*

Materials development

The second part of the network, given in Figure 3.6, shows all the various tasks that should be completed during the materials development phase of the project and its link to the information-gathering phase. This phase, like the previous one, takes approximately 40 hours.

To ensure that this phase of the project runs smoothly an outcomes chart similar to one in Figure 3.7 can be developed.

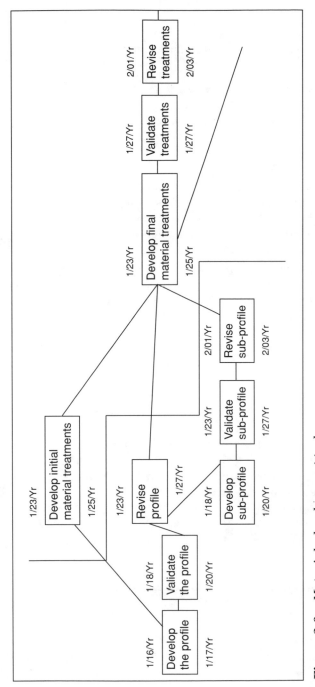

Figure 3.6 *Materials development tasks*

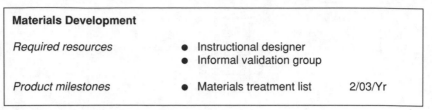

Materials Development		
Required resources	● Instructional designer ● Informal validation group	
Product milestones	● Materials treatment list	2/03/Yr

Figure 3.7   *Products of the materials development phase*

Materials production

The third phase of this project is, in this case, the most complex. Here the network diagram (see Figure 3.8) shows all the various tasks that should be completed during the materials production phase of the project, and its link to the materials development phase. This phase of the project takes approximately 280 hours.

As noted previously two writers have been assigned to the project and will start their respective assignments at the same time. One writer will develop the teacher workbook and the teaching aids, the other, the learner workbook and support materials and all the evaluation materials.

Wherever possible it is to your advantage to have two or more people working on the development of learning materials at the same time. Doing this:

● helps you achieve better continuity and consistency in the materials
● allows people to cross reference each other's work
● allows people to talk about their work and give each other different ideas for the presentation of concepts and the like
● allows people to focus on the job at hand
● keeps people on task.

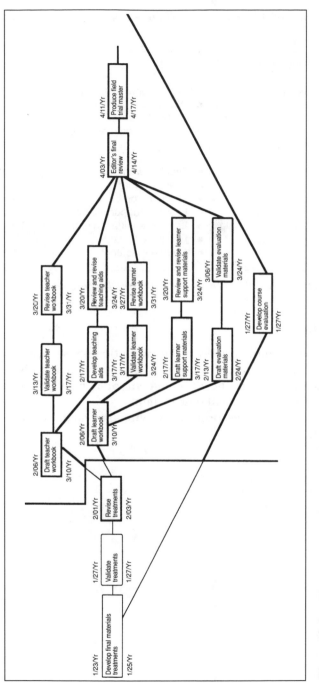

Figure 3.8 *Materials production tasks*

For this phase of the project the outcomes chart would look like Figure 3.9.

Materials Production

Required resources
- Instructional designer
- Writer 1
- Writer 2
- Informal validation group
- Editor

Product milestones
- Teacher workbook   3/31/Yr
- Teacher aids   3/24/Yr
- Learner workbook   3/31/Yr
- Learner support materials   3/24/Yr
- Learner evaluation materials   3/24/Yr
- Editor's final copy   4/14/Yr
- Course master   4/17/Yr

Figure 3.9   *Products of the materials production phase*

Evaluation

Remember to leave enough time for a field trial and make sure that you determine if it is going to be a real time trial or if it will only touch on certain aspects of the materials.

The final phase of the project is the evaluation phase (see Figure 3.10) and takes approximately 28 hours. The actual materials, the final materials review and the development of a master copy are not included as part of the total time estimate.

For this phase of the project the outcomes chart would look like Figure 3.11.

Figure 3.10 *Evaluation tasks*

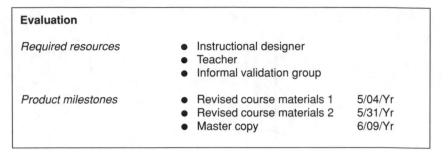

Figure 3.11   *Products of the evaluation phase*

CONCLUSION

This chapter has described the tasks that have to be undertaken if you are to successfully develop your learning materials within a given time limit. As you start the project it is important that you give serious consideration to all the tasks that have to be completed and assign an appropriate time to each one. It has been suggested by some, somewhat tongue in cheek, that whatever time you determine is appropriate to complete a task should be doubled, then a 'fudge factor' added. This could in fact prove to be good advice if you are really in the dark about time allocation for some tasks. It's possible that even with all your hard work your first project will suffer from a miscalculation in time. However, if you have done your homework and have made a serious attempt to time each event, you will very quickly know when you are running into problems. This in itself will save you from costly overruns and allow you to readjust at an early stage so very little damage is done.

It is important that you determine up-front exactly *what* it is that you will be producing and *when* each of those products must be finished. If you don't know what it is you are producing how will you know when it is finished?

Chapter 4

Developing The Learner Profile

SUMMARY

A learner profile can be defined as a block diagram that outlines the various topics that must be learned in order to successfully complete a course. The development of a learner profile is an often exacting process that can, under some circumstances, be completed in a half-day session or it can last as long as two days. Once validated, the learner profile becomes part of the documentation and forms the basis for the development of your learning materials.

This chapter will outline a typical methodology for the development of a learner profile.

THE LEARNER PROFILE

The profile

The development of the learner profile is the next step in the learning materials development process and is based on the initial work you did in the Course Information Document (CID). When it is completed, the profile will outline the various tasks a learner must undertake if they are to 'pass' the course.

A learner profile is made up of a number of rows called 'bands'. Each band has a title box (the first box on the left) that describes the competency or skill the learner is to learn. The title box, for the purpose of this book, can be considered as, or part of, the course goal or aim. In terms of the development of your actual learning materials, you can think of the title box as a chapter heading. Each smaller box in the band, moving from left to right, represents one learning objective

A profile is an outline of what the learners will be learning. Don't use it as an outline of what the teacher will be doing in the classroom!

that helps describe how that goal or aim is to be reached by the learner. In terms of the development of learning materials, each objective can represent one topic. The number of bands in a profile and their size vary according to the materials being developed. A typical profile band is shown in Figure 4.1.

Developing the learner profile	Describing the profile	Planning the profile session	Conducting the profile session	Validating the profile session	Developing the sub-profile
1.0	1.1	1.2	1.3	1.4	1.5

Figure 4.1   *Typical profile band*

The development of a learner profile is similar in procedure to a Developing A Curriculum or DACUM session; here the procedure is less rigid but it provides equally good results.

A profile session is divided into a number of steps as follows.

PLANNING THE PROFILE SESSION

Who should attend the session?

The first step in the development of a profile is to determine who will take part in the session. This can be a task fraught with difficulties. As noticed in Chapter 1, any project centred round the design and development of learning materials has many 'experts' and it is often a delicate matter to ensure all the people involved in the project are working on the task most appropriate to their expertise. You will need to base your choice of people that attend the profile session on their:

- expertise in the field
- position in the organization they represent
- commitment to the methodology being employed
- willingness and ability to discuss the issues surrounding the topics under discussion
- availability to be involved in the session.

Don't let anyone convince you that a 'large' group will help you get the job done more effectively. Large groups are notoriously difficult to work with.

No matter how carefully you select your group it is possible that one or more of them will not be as cooperative during the session as you hoped. The guidelines in Figure 4.2, later in this chapter, will help you deal with some of the problems that can occur during the session.

Determining the size of the group

To ensure a successful profiling session takes place, you will need, ideally, a group of six to nine people. However, to get a group of this size you may find it necessary to have a pool of ten to 15 people to choose from. In some cases you can reduce the size of the group to three to five persons but only if you are sure that the participants you have chosen have the right expertise and the willingness and ability to discuss the various issues surrounding each of the learner topics. Any less than this number is not advisable as you may have validity problems later on.

Selecting the session leader

Early in the planning process it will be necessary for you to determine who will lead the profile session. This person need not be a subject-matter expert and in many cases having someone without expertise in the profile under development can be useful, in that he or she can ask the kind of questions that in other circumstances would not be tolerated. The person you choose should, however, be skilled in group dynamics, be well versed in the process of profile development – including the writing of learning objectives – and have a sound knowledge of pedagogy.

The profile session leader has to be able to lead the group and direct them toward the goal, so make sure that you have the right person for the job.

Session preparation

It is important that each member of your group is well briefed on what will be expected of him or her during the session. Included in your pre-session materials should be:

- a copy of the validated CID
- a guide to the CID and how it is used as part of the documentation
- instructions for the review of the goals and objectives listed in the CID
- a short description of what will take place during the profiling session
- an outline of the role group members will be expected to play during the session.

You should send a package of materials, including instructions for use, to each member of the group at least one week prior to the session being held.

More session preparation

It is essential that you are well prepared for the session by ensuring that enough materials are on hand for the session to continue uninterrupted except for sanctioned breaks. These materials should include two or more packages of large index cards in two colours, a selection of markers, writing paper and at least one (two is better!) packet of Blu-Tack or similar for sticking the cards to a wall without damaging or marking it. An alternative to cards is an electronic whiteboard. Here each band can be written-up using the different 'slates' available and the result printed as the session progresses.

Organizing the room

Whether your group members are from different faculties of the educational community, the industrial sector or some other group in society, you should try to hold the profile session on 'neutral' territory as this will help reduce any feelings of favouritism. It will also allow the group to concentrate on the task at hand without interruptions from the office. You might want to suggest that group members don't bring their pagers or mobile telephones to the sessions.

You will need to carefully check out the room you are going to use and consider each of the following suggestions. It is essential that the room is large enough to seat the group comfortably. Ideally the chairs and tables should be arranged in a U, facing a large blank wall on which the index cards can be placed. The U should be set up with enough space for the group leader to move into the open end when needed, but the sides of the U should be close enough to allow people on each side to interact with ease. If a U set-up is not possible, a board-room-style set-up can be used but only if the group is small enough so that all members of the group can face the group leader and interact with each other. The room should be equipped with a flip chart and/or a portable whiteboard. You might also wish to consider a telephone close by (particularly if you have made the decision to ask participants not to bring theirs along) to allow group members to check in with the office during prescribed breaks.

CONDUCTING THE SESSION

Getting started

Prior to the session starting the group leader should introduce each member of the group, explain the purpose of the session, its expected length and, most importantly, list the expected outcomes. This task is necessary to help all members of the group feel part of the process. Before any profile development can take place it will be necessary for the leader to review each of the goals and objectives listed on the CID and to ensure that they are indeed valid. All changes should be noted on the flip chart. Once the review is complete and all the changes made, all objectives should be listed on the flip chart in full view of the group so that when needed the group leader can direct everyone to the list to ensure the session stays on track.

It should be noticed that if the group asks for major changes to the goals and objectives listed in the CID, there may be a problem with either the group who validated it or the profile group. You would be well-advised at this stage in the development of the documentation to allow the profile group to redraft the goals and objectives of the CID and then develop the profile accordingly. At a later date you can re-validate the CID with a different validation group and hopefully determine where the problem(s) occurred.

Starting a profile session is often a bit chaotic. That's okay – stay focused and you find that things will get on track quite quickly.

Where to begin

Beginning a profile session can be a difficult task as the members of the group are often reluctant to speak and in many cases still do not fully understand what is expected of them. If the session is to get off to a good start the group leader must first explain how each of the major topic headings or band titles are developed and enlist the help, for this part of the session, of one of the group to quickly jot down on the index cards each of the ideas as they are suggested. The group leader should then have the group 'brainstorm' a list of topics appropriate for the materials being developed. It is very important that the group understands that:

If at the start of a profile session you find that the group is heading in the wrong direction, don't be afraid to stop everything, re-explain the goals if necessary, refocus the group and start again.

- the goals and objectives as developed in the CID must be kept in mind
- no particular order for the titles is necessary or should be made at this stage
- there are no 'wrong' answers.

As the various band titles are suggested and quickly jotted down on the index cards, the group leader should stick the cards on to the wall. No attempt should be made to order the cards at this time. The session should continue until the group appears to have exhausted the range of topics. At this point the group leader can ask the participants to review each of the cards and reflect on their appropriateness. As the group is doing this, the group leader should take the opportunity to rewrite any cards difficult to read or where the meaning is not clear because of the need to hurry during brainstorming. No cards should be rewritten to change the meaning in any way without the consent of the group and no cards should be discarded unless approved by the group.

Once the group has been given the opportunity to review the cards the leader should ask the following questions:

● Should any of the cards be removed from the list? (If the answer is yes, the 'removed' cards should be placed on a different portion of the wall as they might be needed at a later time.)
● Can any of the titles be consolidated under one title? (If the answer is yes those cards should be physically placed under the card that appears to be the most representative of the title and a new title written.)

Once this is complete the group should again review the list with a further two questions in mind. These are:

● Does anything else need to be added to the list as it now stands? (If the answer is yes, new cards should be added as appropriate.)
● Is the list of topics in its correct order? (The answer here will, most often, be no; however, the group should be encouraged to spend a few moments to review the list and determine if that is indeed the case.)

Once the group has ordered the topics it will be necessary for the leader to rearrange the cards into a vertical pattern. The list should be in the order that the learning materials will be presented, or the order that the learner will need to learn the materials, if different. If it is appropriate, the leader may wish to introduce the concept of pre- and co-requisites and have the group consider each of these as the list is ordered. The ordering of the list can often take a considerable period of time and a break may be needed before the task is completed. It might also be necessary for the leader to arbitrate differences of opinion regarding the order of the cards by suggesting appropriate alternatives based on knowledge of the audience for the materials, learning theory and the like and/or pointing out the appropriate sections of the CID. It should be noted, however, that the order of the cards should not be considered fixed. As the session continues, it may become apparent that the order needs to change and the leader should be open to making these changes. Once the basic ordering is complete, the group should be instructed on the procedures for developing each of the bands.

The next step

Bands can be developed in any order that the group feels appropriate. Once a band has been chosen for development, however, the group should concentrate on that band and not move from one band to another on an ad hoc basis. Prior to starting, the group leader should review the process for the development of the bands and review the relevant portions of the CID.

When ready, the leader should then have the group consider the band under development and, through discussion, generate a series of topics appropriate for that band. As with the development of the band titles, it is important that the group understand that:

While the profile session is at one level 'freewheeling' it takes a strong session leader to keep things on track and focused. Make sure that you have the right session leader.

● the goals and objectives should be kept in mind
● no particular order for the sub-topics is necessary or should be made
● there are no 'wrong' answers.

As the various topics are suggested, the group leader should write each of them on an index card and stick the card on the wall next to the appropriate band title. Again no attempt should be made to order the cards at this time. Unlike the brainstorming session, the development of the topics will take a significant amount of time and should involve a great deal of discussion. It is important that the leader keeps the group on topic – because of the often wide-ranging nature of the discussion during this part of the session, the group may digress. This can be tolerated for a short time, as it is often seen by the group as a break; however, a certain amount of skill will be needed to get the group back on track without upsetting the interaction that is taking place.

If the group proves to be difficult to get back to the topic at hand, the leader would be wise to call for a break to see if that will help resolve the problem. No matter how the profile group has been chosen, some difficulties may arise; the guidelines in Figure 4.2 may prove helpful.

Situation	Solution
The person who wants to impose their opinion on the whole group. The know-it-all.	Encourage the rest of the group to comment freely on his/her remarks. Let the rest of the group take care of the problem. Build up the confidence of the group so they are not put upon by this type of person.
The person who wants to argue. This type of person is always trying to cross the group leader and will quibble over the most trivial of details and loves to get the rest of the group going.	The first rule in this type of situation is to keep cool. The group leader must not lose his/her cool or allow any other member of the group to do so. Use questions, draw out the individual and turn him/her over to the group. Ensure that any remarks made are not personal. Get the opinion of the majority.
The over-talkative person. The one who has to do all the talking.	Be tactful but interrupt and ask others to comment. It might be necessary to ask the person to refrain from talking and give others a chance. Guide the session. If it can't be done without embarrassing the person, try taking him/her aside during a break. Fail to recognize the person by not looking at him/her and make it difficult for the person to 'get on the floor'. Establish rules so that all those who want to speak get an equal chance.
The shy person.	Ask the person for comments but try to make sure he/she knows the answers; do not put him/her on the spot. Provide a lot of positive feedback. If the person does not want to provide an answer immediately, move on to someone else.
The obstinate person who has no time for all this 'new stuff'.	In a tactful way try to bring the particular part of the session to a close. Pick out something that the person has said and hold it up as a good example.
The uninterested person.	Try to determine his/her likes or dislikes. Pick out something that the person has said and hold it up as a good example.
The person who attempts to get the opinion of the group leader instead of giving his/her own.	Refer the question back to the group and then back to the person.

The person who carries a personal grudge.	Avoid discussion about the person's pet dislike(s). Guide the session. Set rules for the session that state that it must be for the good of all the group and a personal agenda will not be allowed.
The person who is wrong but others in the group will not or can not correct them.	Avoid direct criticism. Try to analyse a different situation without reference to that person. Guide the session to its logical conclusion.

Figure 4.2 *Hints for dealing with difficult people during a profile session*

The session should continue until the group appears to have exhausted the range of topics for that band. It will be necessary for the group leader to ensure that all of the needed sub-topics have been listed. This will require frequent checking with the group in the form of questions such as:

● Does anything else need to be added to the band as it now stands?
   (If the answer is yes, new cards should be added as is appropriate.)
● Can any of the sub-topics be consolidated under one sub-topic?
   (If the answer is yes, those cards should be physically placed under the card that appears to be the most representative of that topic and a new title written.)

It is important to remember that, for the most part, the group leader can ask those questions that appear 'silly' in order to ensure the process proceeds correctly. It is also important to remember that as they are being developed, the topics do not have to be in order; that will be completed later. The group, however, will frequently want to place topics in order as this process often helps many of them determine the next topic title. This need not be discouraged. Once the band appears to be finished, the group leader should again ask which if any items can be consolidated, added or deleted. Again, if the group determines that a topic card should be discarded, that card should not be thrown away but placed to one side ready for use in a different band or replaced in the original band as new considerations are made by the group.

Completing the profile

The process of determining each of the band topics should continue until each is completed. As noted above, this process can take a considerable amount of time and breaks should be provided on a regular basis. However, if the group is working hard on a particular band, the break might be best held when the group appears to have completed the task. Once all the bands are completed, the group should be asked to review each band in turn giving thought to each of the, by now, standard questions. They should also consider whether anything else needs to be added: should any discarded cards be placed back into the profile; and are the sub-topics in the correct order?

The last lap

Profiles are often considered finished once all the topics have been identified. However, two additional tasks should be completed to help ensure the course materials being developed are as correct as possible. The first task is to ask that the group consider, in turn, each of the topics in each band and determine the verb that best describes the action required of the learner to complete that task (see the list given in Figure 4.3). This will help you later in the development of viable objectives. Remember that objectives are useful not only to you as the course developer but also to your learners, as they tell them where they are going, how they are going to get there, and how they will know when they have arrived. A useful objective is one that allows both you and the learner to make the largest number of decisions relevant to its achievement.

The verbs shown in Figure 4.3 are applicable to the various levels in the cognitive domain. You should note that, depending on their use, some verbs may apply to more than one level.

The second task is a little more complex and one that will be discussed in the next chapter of this book. You will find that as you, or a team of writers, try to develop the actual course materials it will be difficult for you to know what should be included in the materials. Take for example a band titled, 'Apply the tools of a quality control circle', with topics such as, 'Define a quality control circle' and, 'Describe the tools of quality control'. As they are written, albeit without conditions and standards, they are fairly typical learning objectives, but they tell you nothing about the learning materials that need to be developed. To help you resolve this problem you will need to complete a sub-profile sheet.

Knowledge		Comprehension	
arrange	order	classify	locate
define	recognize	describe	recognize
duplicate	recall	discuss	report
label	relate	explain	restate
list	repeat	express	review
memorize	reproduce	identify	select
name		indicate	translate

Application		Analysis	
apply	operate	analyse	differentiate
choose	practise	appraise	discriminate
demonstrate	schedule	calculate	distinguish
dramatize	sketch	categorize	examine
employ	solve	compare	experiment
illustrate	use	contrast	question
interpret		criticize	test

Synthesis		Evaluation	
arrange	formulate	appraise	evaluate
assemble	manage	argue	judge
collect	organize	assess	predict
compose	plan	attach	rate
construct	prepare	choose	score
create	propose	compare	select
design	set up	defend	support
	write	estimate	value

Figure 4.3   *Verbs appropriate to each of the levels of the cognitive domain*

Once the profile is completed by the group in the profiling session the group leader should number all the cards before removing them from the wall. A common numbering system uses a whole number for the band title, ie, 1, and a decimal number for each of the topics, ie, 1.1. Once numbered, the cards can be removed and a written profile developed using a format similar to the band shown in Figure 4.1. It is possible that at this stage you will have to make minor changes for the sake of clarity; you should remember, however, that no major changes should be made without consultation with the group as a whole. Once you have completed the profile it should be prepared ready for validation.

VALIDATION

Preparation

Validation is a very important step in the profile process. Don't be tempted *not* to make it part of the overall process.

Preparing the profile for validation involves three steps:

- preparing the instructions for the validation group
- selecting the validation group
- revising the profile according to the findings of the validation group.

You will need to spell out clearly the instructions for the validation process so the group members are in no doubt as to the procedure they must follow. The validation package could include a blank profile to allow additional topics to be added by the validator.

You can use two methods to validate the profile. The most simple and direct method is to send it out to a newly-selected group or the original profile group if a new group is not available or warranted, or if that is the most appropriate action for the project. The profile has to be reviewed, checked for errors and the various topics assessed for appropriateness to the subject under discussion. As the profiles are returned, they should be reviewed for changes and suggestions and a revised profile developed. This updated version can then be sent out for final confirmation or can be used as it is to begin the development of the learning materials.

CONCLUSION

This chapter has described the procedure that should be followed when developing a learner profile. The task can be a frustrating one and it will take a lot of skill to get the right product. The key to getting the profile right the first time is to ensure you get the right mix of people in the profile group. Be very selective, even if the pool of talent you have available to you is very small. Make sure that your group members know what is expected of them before they start the profiling session and make sure they have at least some commitment to the systematic process of learning materials development.

Ensure that you review the CID and that its goals and objectives are clear with respect to the profile being developed. Be firm but fair with the group and ensure that they stay on track as much as possible – keep checking. A final hint, if the profile is stalled and the group members are getting restless and seem unwilling to take the session to its conclusion. Try asking one of the participants, perhaps the one who is forever talking, to take over from whoever is leading the group and see if he or she can get the job finished. This person will take some persuading (it's part of the game) but he or she will eventually get up and 'take over'. In most cases this will break the deadlock and the group will like the change and respond positively. The resulting product will possibly not be worth much in terms of the profile itself, but it does get things moving again.

Chapter 5
Developing The Learner Sub-profile

SUMMARY

As with the course profile, the sub-profile can be defined as a block diagram. However, the sub-profile goes one step further and outlines for the writer(s) or the developers of the learning materials the various topic headings that have to be covered to ensure the learner reaches his or her appropriate level of learning.

This chapter will outline a typical methodology for the development of a sub-profile.

INTRODUCTION

A sub-profile, like the main profile, is made up of a number of rows called 'bands' whose length and complexity can vary, depending upon the materials you are developing. The development of a sub-profile is the second and final stage of the profile development described in the previous chapter. The sub-profile can be developed using three methodologies. It can be completed:

● at the end of the main profile session
● by each member of the profile group individually after the profile session has ended
● as part of the validation process by the validation group.

Which ever way it is done, the purpose of the sub-profile is twofold: when you are writing learning materials it will serve as a guide to what materials have to be written; when you are determining both general and specific learning objectives and the various steps needed for the learner to achieve those specific objectives, the sub-profile is an important information tool.

DEVELOPING THE SUB-PROFILE

Some developers of learning materials see the development of the sub-profile as too difficult and too much trouble. They like to stop after the main profile and complete a series of validation steps to determine general and specific learning objectives, or if they are writing learning materials, they will start writing and validate the topic once it is finished. The problem with both of these methods is that you can get a long way off track before being told that what is being developed is not correct. This upsets both budgets and time lines, not to mention the writers!

The profile and the sub-profile can be used as the basis for the development of all types of learning materials. For the purposes of this discussion we will consider the example introduced in the previous chapter (see Figure 4.1); it could, however, just as easily have been part of a video script or part of the instructional sequence developed for a computer-based lesson. You should appreciate that this profile band, shown again in Figure 5.1, is useful as it gives you big hints as to what is needed by the learner; however, it does not describe what actually has to be developed.

Developing the learner profile	Describing the profile	Planning the profile session	Conducting the profile session	Validating the profile session	Developing the sub-profile
1.0	1.1	1.2	1.3	1.4	1.5

Figure 5.1 *Typical profile band*

The sub-profile, on the other hand, outlines for you each of the various parts of each profile band. In the example in Figure 5.2, each sub-topic of box 1.2, *Planning the profile session*, has been determined and all the various items that will have to be written under that sub-topic have been itemized.

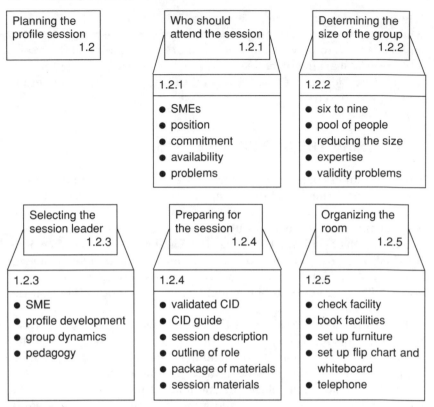

Figure 5.2   *Typical sub-profile band (1)*

The sub-profile can also be used as the basis for the development of specific learning objectives. In this example, box 1.2, *Planning the profile session,* can now be considered as a general learning objective and each sub-section a specific learning objective. The topics listed under each sub-section then become the steps the learner will have to take to reach that specific learning objective.

Objectives that will have to be incorporated into your learning materials under headings such as telling learners what they need to learn, showing learners how those things are done and having learners practise the skills they need to achieve competence, are shown in Figure 5.3.

Figure 5.3 *Typical sub-profile band (2)*

COMPLETING THE SUB-PROFILE

Completing the sub-profile during the main profile session

Like the profile itself, the sub-profile can be a time-consuming process that will demand all the skills of the group leader if the task is to be correctly completed. It is possible that if the group was not prepared to complete this extra task at the start of the session, the leader will have a difficult time getting participants motivated.

Once the profile has been reviewed, the leader will need to determine where the group would like to start to develop the sub-profile. Profile cards should not be removed from the wall as they are needed to guide the group. A new card should be written out for each topic that needs to be expanded and placed on an appropriate blank portion of the wall. Wherever the group decides to start, the leader should ask the group to list the sub-topics contained under each topic. This should follow a similar pattern to the development of the original profile, with various members of the group making suggestions as needed and the group leader writing the cards, asking questions and making sure the session is productive. The new cards can be set up on one side of the profile ready to be numbered and collected after the session is finished.

As with the profile, once discussion of the sub-topics seems finished, the leader should ask the group to review the cards and ask the standard questions regarding removing any cards from the list and consolidating any of them under one title. Further questions will need to be asked regarding any additions to the list and the ordering of the cards. Once it has been determined that the sub-topics are correct, the leader needs to decide what items should be made part of each of them. Determining the items can be very difficult in a group setting and it is recommended that participants are not asked to complete this task. Topics can be determined by the course developer and validated along with the profile, or the validation group can be asked to complete them.

The session should continue until all the sub-topics are determined and the group is satisfied with the result. It should be noted that both the group and its leader will have to be task-oriented to get the sub-profile completed at the end of the profile session.

Completing the sub-profile after the session is over

A second method for determining the sub-profile is to have it completed by the profile group *after* the formal session is over. However, to do this the group leader will have to explain in detail what has to be done and provide the group with an example and a template for them to complete. The group will also need a copy of the profile. This will mean that immediately upon finishing the main profile session it will have to be typed up and sent to the group along with the template and a description of what has to be done. Two methods can be used to complete this task: all of the group can be asked to complete all of the profile, or prior to people leaving the profile session, bands can be assigned to various members of the group. The second method is advisable if the profile is a large one. A strict deadline should be placed on the completion of the sub-profile, with telephone follow-up as the deadline approaches. Once the sub-profile(s) is returned, it and the profile itself can be put together ready for validation.

Completing the sub-profile during validation

The third method is to use the validation group. Here you prepare the profile and have it validated using the technique described in the validation section of Chapter 4. Trying to develop a sub-profile if you are using the Delphi technique for validation would not be advisable as it would take too long and would be an imposition on the group. Once the validation of the main profile is complete, group members are asked to describe the sub-topics. This can be completed in a formal session just like the profile session itself, or it can be carried out on an individual basis. Whichever method is used, the task will have to be explained in detail and, if it's an individual effort, templates provided ready for completion.

CONCLUSION

Like the development of the profile, getting the sub-profile ready to be a viable part of the course documentation can be an arduous task. It is important to remember that the development of the sub-profile can be carried out using one of three methodologies. It is possible, however, that a final decision on that methodology will not be made until the profile session is coming to an end. In many cases, leaving the decision to this point is appropriate as the group leader will be better able to judge the ability of the profile group to continue into the sub-profile phase. Whatever methodology is being considered, it should be carried out in a systematic way and added to the documentation ready for use by the writers of the learning materials.

Chapter 6
Writing Learning Objectives

SUMMARY

A useful objective is one that allows the teacher to make the largest number of decisions relevant to its achievement and measurement. A meaningful objective is one that communicates intent by excluding the greatest number of possible meanings other than what is intended.

   This chapter describes the development of objectives and their uses in both learning and learning materials.

INTRODUCTION

Objectives are useful in the design, implementation and evaluation of instruction. They tell your learners where they are going and how they are going to get there. They tell you how you will know when the learners have arrived.

   Objectives, in order to communicate the exact intent, should be written using phrases that are open to as few interpretations as possible (see Mager, 1975 for further information). For example:

Words open to many interpretations	Words open to fewer interpretations
know	arrange
understand	label
become comfortable with	describe

appreciate	review
fully appreciate	apply
grasp the significance of	solve
enjoy	calculate
believe	contrast
have faith in	design
internalize	formulate
recognize	evaluate

Different responses may be expected from learners when certain action verbs are used. For further information see, for example, Grunland 1976.

Objectives consist of as many statements, items or examples as are necessary to describe the desired behaviour of learners at the time they leave your course or some other learning event. Objectives should be prepared in enough detail so all teachers could, if it were necessary, turn out learners to all do the same things.

WHAT ARE OBJECTIVES?

Objectives describe the kind of performance expected by the learner at the end of a course or learning event. For example, while highly skilled people may be able to perform a particular task quickly without using job aids to remind them of the steps, it is unrealistic to expect a learner to be able to perform the same task in the same way. It is more realistic to expect the learner to be able to perform all of the steps, determine if the job has been carried out correctly and then correct it if it has not. In this case the learner has the knowledge and the skills to be able to practise the task to improve his/her efficiency.

When developing objectives the key question you must ask yourself is: *What kind of things should learners be able to do at the end of the course or learning event that will most help them become as skilled as possible in the least amount of time?*

A well-written learning objective represents a clear statement of instructional intent and it can be written in any form as long as it clarifies that intent.

The development of learning objectives often leads to insights about the purpose, content and delivery methods of the learning materials. Materials that once seemed important may be discovered to be redundant, or you may find that important concerns have been left out of your materials, or what was being done during the learning event has little or no relation to the objectives that have been developed. It is important to understand that objectives are not set in stone. You may find that as you gain fresh insights into the purpose and methods for the delivery of your learning materials your view of the course goals and the objectives will also change.

As a way of checking if your objectives are appropriate use the following checklist to make sure your objective statements have the necessary characteristics.

Never regard objectives as being final. Typically, they are subject to change.

- An objective says something about your learner. It does **not** describe a textbook, or you as the teacher, or the kinds of learning experience to which the learner will be exposed.
- An objective describes the behaviour or performance of the learner. It does **not** describe the performance of the teacher, nor what the learner is expected to know or understand. Though you might begin an objective using a general statement such as, 'the learner must understand the operation of XYZ machine' you would go on to explain what you mean by 'understand' and to describe what the learner will be expected to do to demonstrate that understanding. Whatever is meant by understanding would be defined in the sentences following the general one. However, to make things easier for yourself, use a verb such as 'describe' or in this case 'demonstrate', where the learner can demonstrate various operations on XYZ machine.

Always start your objective using a verb.

- An objective is about ends rather than means. It describes a product rather than a process. As such it describes what the learner is expected to be able to do at the end of the learning event rather than the means that will be used to get them there. An objective talks about end performance rather than learning materials content.
- An objective describes the conditions under which the learner will be performing the end behaviour. In some cases the learner will be expected to perform in the absence of any assistance provided by job aids.
- An objective should also include information about the level of performance considered acceptable. If the learner is expected to perform a task within a five minute time frame at the end of the instruction, that should be stated as part of the objective. If the performance is expected to be error free or if some error will be tolerated, this should also be indicated.

Useful objectives answer the following questions:

- What should the learner be able to do?
- Under what conditions should the learner be able to do it?
- How well must the performance be carried out?

Objectives should be written so that they specify the following:

Performance: what the learner is expected to do
Conditions: the important conditions under which the performance is to occur
Standards: the minimum criteria that the learner must meet in order for his or her performance to be acceptable.

Performance

Performance refers to any activity engaged in by the learner. It can be a visible performance such as writing, sorting, or labelling, or it can be invisible such as reviewing or solving.

The way to write an objective that includes performance is to write a statement that answers this question: 'What is the learner doing when demonstrating achievement of the objective?'

For example an objective written in performance terms might appear as follows:

Define a virtual circuit.

The main intent of this objective is simply for the learner to define a virtual circuit. It is not clear if the learner is to define the circuit orally or in writing, but what is clear is what is expected of the learner when he or she is demonstrating achievement of the objective. The same is true for the following objective.

Explain the difference between a PNC and a SNC junction.

Again, what is not made clear is how the explanation is to be made, but the expected performance of the learner is clear. The learner has to be able to explain something. Because of the way in which these objectives are written, they are measurable. The quality of a definition or explanation can be measured in a number of different ways. Quite often, however, this type of objective is written using the verb 'understand'. Unfortunately, when an objective is written in this fashion, for example 'understand a virtual circuit', it becomes very difficult, if not impossible, to measure how much, if anything, the learner has learned about virtual circuits.

Most objectives can be written in just performance terms.

Conditions

Conditions refer to those things imposed on the learners when they are demonstrating their mastery of the objective. Consider these examples.

- Given a problem of the following type ...
- Given a list of ...
- Given any reference of the learner's choice ...
- Given a map of ...
- Given a standard set of tools ...
- Given a correctly functioning ...
- Without the aid of references ...
- Without the aid of a calculator ...
- Without the aid of tools ...

An objective that includes conditions is a statement that identifies the important aspects of the target or end performance and answers the following questions.

- What will the learner be allowed to use?
- What will the learner be denied?
- Under what conditions will the behaviour occur?
- Are there any skills that are not to be developed and does the objective exclude those skills?

Determining the conditions for an objective will help you when it comes to writing your test questions.

Consider the following performance objective.

Without the aid of references write three equations for determining the power dissipated in a typical electrical circuit.

Once again the intent, or performance, has been made clear: the learner has to write three equations. The conditions are also very clear. He or she has to write those three equations without the aid of references.

Consider also the following, more complex, performance objective.

Given a list of appropriate equations, select the correct equation and calculate the current in any simple circuit in which two of the following quantities are known: power, resistance, voltage.

In this objective the learner is being asked first to select the correct equation to solve a particular mathematical problem and next use that equation to make a calculation. Again, the conditions have been clearly stated: the learner is to be given a list of equations from which he or she is to make a selection. Other conditions have also been spelled out such as the known quantities of the circuit, which in this case are power, resistance and voltage.

Standards

Standards refer to how well a learner has to perform and is the yardstick by which achievement of the objective is assessed. Standards are set to specify a desired criterion. For example, an acceptable performance could be marginal or must be perfect, depending on the circumstances of the action. The most common way to describe standards is to use time or accuracy. For example:

When an objective becomes lengthy and complex break it up into two or even three different parts.

> Given a computer and using appropriate word processing software, prepare a standard business letter consistent with business format MR54. The letter should comprise three paragraphs of no more than 100 words each, with no spelling or typographical errors and should be completed in 20 minutes or less.

Objectives can include standards such as:

● ... accurate to the nearest whole number
● ... accurate to the nearest gramme
● ... three significant figures
● ... no more than three incorrect entries for every page in the log.

Consider the following two objectives.

> Given a standard four cylinder petrol engine exhibiting five malfunctions, and being told one symptom for each malfunction, be able to locate each malfunction in ten minutes or less.

and

> Given a compass, ruler, pencil and paper, be able to construct and bisect any given angle larger than 10° accurate to the nearest degree.

As you can see, the objectives each contain a performance, a condition and a standard. In the first objective the expected performance the learner is to exhibit is to locate a number of engine malfunctions, the conditions under which the performance is to take place involves a standard four cylinder petrol engine that exhibits a number of malfunctions and the learner is expected to locate each of the malfunctions in ten minutes or less.

In the second objective the learner is expected to be able to construct and bisect a given angle larger than 10°. He or she may use a compass, ruler, pencil and paper to aid in the task and to complete the activity accurate to within one degree.

Objectives written in this form make test question development less difficult and help in the development of viable learning materials.

EDITING EXISTING OBJECTIVES

Whenever you develop learning materials ready for delivery to the learner, typically you will make two assumptions. First, you assume that the product of the delivery of those materials to the learner will result in a change to that learner. Second, you assume that in selecting the means by which to change the learner you can do a better job if you state precisely what you will accept as evidence of competence in the learner. As has been discussed previously, you know that a learning objective should describe what learners will be able to do when they have been changed in the desired way. However, not all objectives are written in a way that aids learners in accomplishing what needs to be accomplished as they work through various parts of the learning materials.

It is important, therefore, that you are able to recognize well-stated objectives and edit poorly stated ones.

Consider the following objective.

Typically poorly written objectives begin with the words 'The student will understand ...'

Write an essay describing the causes of World War I. The essay must demonstrate an understanding of the more subtle forces leading up to the war and an appreciation of historical relationships.

At first glance it appears to be appropriate. It has a fairly well-described intent and appears to have a well-described standard. However, on closer review it becomes evident that it is not well written. For example, it is difficult, if not impossible to measure 'demonstrate an understanding' and 'an appreciation of historical relationships'.

Here the learner would be better served if the objective was edited to read as follows.

> The essay must describe in detail each of the various forces that combined to bring about the war and further describe their historical relationship.

This edited version, albeit not perfect, does help make the objective measurable. From the test question that can be derived from this objective, a comprehensive marking scheme can also be developed to aid the person marking the question more accurately grade the quality of the written answer.

Consider also this objective.

> Given a functioning, but poorly adjusted, acquisition amplifier, adjust it within a five minute time period, so that it tracks and locks correctly.

This objective can stand on its own. It describes the learner performance (adjusting the amplifier so it tracks and locks correctly), has a set of conditions (a functioning, but poorly adjusted, acquisition amplifier) and it sets out a time based standard of performance (within five minutes). Again the objective is not perfect but it does clearly specify the intent and is focused on the learner.

For the most part you should be able to list the characteristics of a well-written objective. Even if you are not familiar with the subject matter you should be able to decide if the objective format is acceptable. However, if you are not competent in the subject matter, you may find it hard to determine the criteria for acceptable performance.

Keep asking yourself 'What will my learners be able to do when they have achieved this objective?'

Even when you do have such competence, the criteria may be debatable. If, for example, somebody says that they will accept 90 per cent accuracy as evidence of proficiency, what does this mean? Presumably that person is saying that they expect a high level of performance but why is 90 per cent the right number? Why not 75 or 80 or even 65 per cent? Haggling over such details can consume a great deal of time and even be counter productive. Consider the following when you are trying to determine a suitable performance criteria.

- Sometimes 100 per cent is not the only acceptable criterion. However, you would like to think that the surgeon removing your gall bladder had been trained to 100 per cent, or the pilot of the plane you are in and just about to land at a small landing strip in the middle of the Amazon jungle had received 100 per cent in landing procedures.

● Often, however, 100 per cent is not a realistic criterion. The person being tested may not have complete control over all the variables that affect the performance. Perfection may not matter. Competent learners often make 'silly' mistakes under the pressure of a test. Some mistakes are more acceptable than others.

● Some criteria are expandable. A learner may perform all of the steps in an operation successfully but the actual performance might be slower than someone with more experience. If time is not an issue, then allow a long time limit or do not use one at all.

● Sometimes the only way to arrive at a criterion is to make it up and see if it fits the case. If it is appropriate in the learning situation then let it be, if it appears to be too high or too low adjust it accordingly until it appears right.

All too often what is actually achieved during the learning event and what you hoped to achieve are not the same. Often there are gaps in the instruction, holes that appear because you are the expert in the subject.

Sometimes you inadvertently allow assumptions to creep into the development of materials or you find that the materials 'teach' one thing while the objective calls for something else. One of the most common examples of this is instruction that teaches learners to *talk* about something while the objective calls for them to *do* something.

Such problems are understandable. As the expert who speaks the language of whatever business you are in it's easy to forget that learners are not equally familiar with the jargon or comfortable with the way in which it is used and the experienced viewpoint it represents.

When you are in the process of developing objectives as part of your learning materials you need to be able to review the learning materials and to derive from these materials a good idea of what is to be expected from that instruction.

If you are in the process of reviewing materials with a view to revising them you will need to look at the materials and compare them with current objectives and perhaps develop new and different objectives.

One way to proceed is to review the materials and develop the objectives that might reasonably be accomplished by learners who work with that material. Doing this will tell you if the instruction is relevant to the objectives and it also tells you something about the relevancy of the objectives to that instruction. A final strategy is to review the tests and determine what outcomes are considered important.

As a short exercise read the following passage. When you have finished write down what you think might be the chief performance(s) you would expect of the learner (whose studies were limited to these passages). Do not write objectives with conditions and standards. Just identify the performance.

Your learning objectives should be determined from your learner profile.

Making beef stock

Stock for the soup may be made from meat, fish or poultry.

You cannot rush the preparation of stock, so pick a day when your soup kettle can sit on the back of the stove, murmuring to itself, for several hours. For there is only one way to extract every last subtle bit of flavour, and that is to simmer, simmer, simmer, long and slow, never permitting the stock to come to a full boil.

The beef is chopped up into small pieces, and to give your stock that rich brown colour, begin by browning the meat in the kettle, using marrow fat scraped from the bones. Add water and your favourite seasonings – salt for sure, perhaps pepper, parsley, thyme, bay and marjoram. Then bring the whole thing slowly to a boiling point and simmer until the aroma nearly drives your taste buds crazy. When all is done, strain the hot stock through a colander and, if you want to use the stock right away, remove some of the fat by skimming the top of the liquid with paper towels.

There are at least six performances in this exercise!

Matching test items to your objectives

Follow the steps listed below to help you match test questions to your course content and objectives.

Step one: analyse the objective

Review each objective and identify the conditions, performance and standard(s) each objective covers.

Step two: write the question

Write at least one test question based on the objective that you think will show that the learner has learned the objective.

Step three: analyse the question

Apply the same analysis to the test question that you gave the objective and determine the conditions, performance and standards.

Step four: compare the question and objective

Compare the test question to the objective and determine if the content is the same.

Step five: revise the question and/or the objective

Where there is a discrepancy between the objective and the test question, revise the question.

DEVELOPING OBJECTIVES FROM TEST ITEMS

As you are aware, there are a number of sources from which you can draw information for the development of learning materials. One such source is test items. Existing learning materials often have previously developed test items that are administered at the end of the instruction. If you derive objectives from these items you will be able to determine what competencies are being taught. Having done that you can make a reasonable decision regarding which objectives should be discarded, which should be kept and which should be rewritten.

One note of caution, however. Typically, many test items are made purposely 'hard' to test a learner's 'skill' and this is not necessarily typical of the desired performance required of the learner. Remember that:

The best way to develop test items is from the learning objectives rather than the other way round.

- the test is probably incomplete if it is regarded as an instrument for assessing desired competence
- it probably seeks a higher level of performance than is truly desired in at least some of its items.

Because of these issues you should be cautious when developing objectives from test items.

When you are developing objectives from test items, the key question to ask yourself is: 'If the learners answer these questions correctly, what can I reasonably expect them to be able to do?'

- Note the performance called for by each of the items having to do with the same subject or skill.
- Decide which is the highest level or the most complex of the performances.

● Draft your objectives first to describe the most complex skills needed for each topic area.
● Draft your objectives to describe the subordinate skills.

Once you have done this you are in a position to ask the following questions.

● Are these performances the ones I want my learners to demonstrate?
● Are there some subordinate objectives missing? Do I need to add objectives describing some subordinate skills that are steps to the performance I want my learners to demonstrate?

Table 6.1 *Expected learner response for selected action verbs*

Action verb	Types of response	Sample test task
Identify	Point to, touch, mark circle, match, pick up	Put an X next to the triangle
Name	Supply verbal label	What is this type of angle called?
Distinguish between	Identify as separate or different by marking, separating into classes, or selecting out the common kind	Which of the following statements are facts (circle F) and which are opinions (circle O)?
Define	Supply a verbal description (orally or in writing) that gives the precise meaning or essential qualities	Define each of the following terms
Describe	Supply a verbal account (orally or in writing) that gives the essential categories, properties and relationships	Describe the procedure for measuring relative humidity in the atmosphere
Classify	Place into groups having common characteristics; assign to a particular category	Write the name of the type of pronoun used in each of the following sentences
Order	List in order, place in sequence, arrange, rearrange	Arrange the following historical events in chronological order
Construct	Draw, make, design assemble, prepare, build	Draw a bar graph using the following data
Demonstrate	Perform a set of procedures with or without a verbal explanation	Set up the laboratory equipment for this experiment

OBJECTIVES CHECKLIST

The following checklist is intended as a tool for detecting and correcting any errors in your final list of objectives. Any negative answer indicates an area where improvement is needed. The checklist is also useful as a guide for developing your original list of objectives.

- Does each general objective indicate an appropriate outcome for the topic?
- Does the list of general objectives include all logical outcomes of the topic?
- Are the general objectives attainable? (Do they take into account the ability of the learners, facilities and time available, for example?)
- Do the objectives exhibit the principles of learning? (Are the outcomes those that are permanent and transferable?)
- Does each general objective begin with a verb?
- Is each general objective stated in terms of learner performance?
- Is each general objective stated as a learning product (rather than a learning process)?
- Is each general objective stated in terms of learner's end behaviour (rather than the subject matter to be covered)?
- Does each general objective include only one learning outcome?
- Is each general objective stated at the correct level of generality? (Is it clear, concise and definable?)
- Is each general objective stated so that it is relatively independent (free from overlap with other objectives)?

CONCLUSION

The development of learning objectives is a task whose importance should not be overlooked. A complete objective contains a learner performance, the condition(s) under which the performance takes place and the standards of performance. However, an objective can be stated in performance terms only and still be viable for use in learning materials.

Chapter 7

Delivery Options: Instructional Strategies and Materials

SUMMARY

This chapter discusses two of the common assumptions made about the way that learning materials can be delivered. These are: there is only one type of instructional strategy, and one kind of support or instructional material. Also discussed are the three basic types of instructional strategies, along with their advantages and disadvantages. Finally, the chapter describes a methodology to help you select the most appropriate type of instructional materials.

INTRODUCTION

Once the learning materials have been planned and the goals and objectives identified, the next step is to determine how you are going to deliver the learning materials and what you will need to assist you as far as support materials are concerned. There are many ways of delivering learning materials to the learner, including lectures, tutorials, class discussions, practical sessions, distance learning, buzz groups, seminars and computer-based learning. Some teachers often find it difficult to select the most appropriate delivery strategy and to know exactly what type of instructional materials to use. This chapter will simplify this choice for you by suggesting a number of simple but effective methods that can assist you to make decisions about the delivery of your learning materials and the other instructional materials that you can use to assist you.

THE COMMON ASSUMPTIONS

A common assumption made regarding the delivery of learning materials is that there is only one delivery and one instructional methodology that can be used. Typically, most people new to the business of delivering learning materials tend to deliver them in the same way that they were taught, and when instructional technology is used, it is often used poorly. For example, the overhead projector is so misused that some learners have coined the phrase, 'Death by overhead'.

As teachers you will need to develop the necessary skills to allow you to use the appropriate delivery method and instructional materials. Try designing your learning materials to include more than one type of delivery strategy and other types of instructional material. Remember, however, that you must make sure that the method you choose is appropriate for your learners.

TYPES OF INSTRUCTIONAL STRATEGY

There are only three types of instruction, so it is very important that you choose the right one.

Lectures, tutorials, workshops, distance-learning, open learning, computer-based instruction, flexible learning, resource-based learning, mastery learning, programme learning, self-help groups, role plays, action learning, competency-based training and interactive video learning can all be categorized into the three basic types of instructional strategy, shown in Figure 7.1.

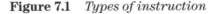

Figure 7.1   *Types of instruction*

When you are planning the delivery of your learning materials there are three types of instructional strategies you can choose from. Within each category your choice becomes difficult as there are a wide number of delivery strategies you can use for your course. 'Delivery strategy' (or 'delivery technique') is defined here as 'the arrangement of or procedures for actually delivering the learning'. It is your broad plan that you will use to direct the learning.

For example, if you choose mass instruction as the instructional strategy for delivering the learning event, the delivery strategy might be the lecture. If you choose individualized instruction as your instructional strategy you could deliver the materials using resource-based or programme learning. So, although there are a limited number of instructional strategies there are many different strategies for delivery.

Mass instruction

Mass instruction is the type of instruction you are probably most familiar with, where the information is provided to a large number of learners by the teacher in person. The same information could also be delivered through broadcast television, video or film. Here the teacher is directly in control of the learning situation but the learning is generally passive. This type of instruction is called 'teacher-centred' because teachers are in control of the instructional process. Some of the various delivery strategies associated with this method of instruction are shown in Figure 7.2.

Figure 7.2 *Typical mass instructional delivery strategies*

The advantages of mass instruction

There are a number of advantages to using mass instruction. These include:

● up-to-date information can be given to the learners quickly and at the same time

- learners quickly get an overview of a subject or topic
- learners can be motivated by an exciting presentation
- its suitability when the content of the course changes constantly
- most teachers and learners are familiar with it
- it's cost-effective
- it makes the logistics of delivering learning materials easy
- the instruction can be given by an acknowledged 'expert' in the field
- the content of the materials can be controlled
- the pace of the delivery is controlled
- a wide variety of instructional materials can be used.

The advantages of mass instruction can also be disadvantages, so choose carefully.

It must be remembered that some of these advantages can also be disadvantages. For example, instead of providing learners with the latest information, teachers may deliver the same material year after year, not taking into account changes that may have occurred.

The disadvantages of mass instruction

There is a movement towards other methods of instruction because of the disadvantages of mass instruction. These disadvantages include:

- its inability to take into account different learning rates or styles of learning
- the passive nature of the learning environment
- the time and location of the event is determined by the teacher
- the number of learning materials that are not suitable for this type of instruction
- its unsuitability for some teaching styles.

Mass instruction delivery strategies

Try to ensure that your lectures are interactive by adding a variety of things for the learner to do.

Despite its many disadvantages the lecture still persists, but now teachers are making them more interactive. This means involving the learner more so that their role is not so passive. Teachers are also using a wider range of teaching aids to help them deliver the lecture.

The lecture can be made more interactive by using a variety of methods, some of which include:

- having a skeletal outline of the lecture that requires completion by the learner
- placing questions in the notes for the learners to answer during the class

- verbally questioning the learners during the class
- forming learners into small groups to answer questions.

If you choose to use the lecture as your delivery method, you should, where appropriate, use teaching aids and design the lecture so that it involves the learner.

Group instruction

Group instruction is where groups of approximately 30 learners work together with the teacher. Here the teacher's role is that of facilitator or organizer in the teaching/learning process.

The tutorial is a typical example of group instruction. Here a problem is set and the teacher assists the learners to solve that problem. This type of delivery strategy is particularly suitable for the achievement of higher order cognitive skills. The teacher sets the problem or task, provides the learning materials, and actively involves the learner. Group instruction is more learner-centred than mass instruction, and better meets the needs of most learners.

The type of delivery strategies associated with group instruction are shown in Figure 6.3. Remember that the content of the course helps determine the delivery method used.

Remember that group instruction is suitable for the achievement of higher order cognitive skills.

The advantages of group instruction

There are many advantages to group instruction, including:

- allowing the achievement of higher order cognitive skills such as synthesis and analysis
- the development of attitudinal skills
- the active involvement of the learner
- allowing the learners to interact and learn from one another
- the use of small amounts of learning materials
- allowing the learner to work in an environment similar to the real world
- having learners work at the pace of the small group
- the use of a variety of teaching and learning materials.

The disadvantages of group instruction

The disadvantages to group instruction include:

- the small numbers involved which often suggests to administrators that it is less cost-effective than mass instruction

Try not to lecture for more than 15 to 30 minutes at one time and always try to include some type of activity that the learners can complete individually or in small groups.

Figure 7.3   *Typical group instruction delivery strategies*

- the pacing of the instruction is still group-based
- the role of the teacher not being clearly defined
- the need for 'special' facilities to follow for small group activities, such as the ability move both chairs and desks so learners can work in small groups
- the more time-consuming nature of the learning event compared to the amount of material covered.

When terms like 'cost-effective' and 'time-consuming' are used in education, you should remember that it is difficult to compare educational effectiveness and the quality of learning. For example, it may be both cost- and time-effective to lecture to 1,000 learners, but the learners may learn very little: in terms of the objectives of educating the learners, the lecture is both cost- and time-inefficient.

When considering your delivery strategy ask yourself which is more important, cost effectiveness or the effectiveness of the learning?

Individualized instruction

Individualized instruction has many viable delivery strategies that include distance learning, open learning, flexible learning, resource-based learning and programme learning. Individualized instruction is defined as, 'the planning of instruction to meet the individual needs and abilities of the learner and take into account their individual differences'.

Individualized instruction is a learner-centred delivery strategy where the teacher acts as a facilitator of the learning process. Here learning materials play an even more important role in the learning process as teachers cannot meet the needs of each individual learner. So the learners learn from materials and the teacher manages their learning in a variety of ways. As you plan for individualized instruction you will need to take into account the many differences between learners. Some of these differences include:

Individualized instruction is learner centred *not* teacher centred. Make sure that your individualized materials are learner focused.

- rates of learning and learning style
- ethnic, cultural, socio-economic, personal beliefs
- attitude
- interests which affect the level of learning
- maturity level
- literacy and numeracy abilities
- needs arising from the instruction itself
- mental abilities, reasoning, creativity and remembering skills
- motivation to learn
- learning environment
- psychomotor skill development.

There are probably many other differences between learners that affect learning, but what is clear is that no two learners are the same. So, attempting to accommodate these differences in mass instruction is very difficult. One of the better ways of handling learning difficulties is by using a learner-centred approach, such as individualized instruction.

Two points need to be made about individualized instruction before proceeding further. First, it can be said that all learning is individualized, be it mass or group instruction, as learners have to do the learning themselves. Only the instruction, the way the teacher assists the learners to learn, can be individualized.

Second, many teachers think that individualized learning means that the learner learns in isolation, in the 'comfort of their own home', as is often the case with distance learners. This may indeed be the

Remember that for the most part all learning is an individual activity and build that into your design.

Individualized learning does not necessarily mean learning in isolation. Learners need interaction for a number of reasons, so build some interaction into your materials.

case, but some forms of individualized instruction can take place in a group environment. For example, the learners are in a class where there are using instructional materials under the guidance of the teacher, but all are working at their own pace on different topics.

Effective individualized learning materials should include group activities with appropriate points of interaction between learners and teachers.

The advantages of individualized instruction

There are a number of advantages for the learners in an individualized learning setting using group activities. For example:

● they can learn from each other
● expensive or scarce resources can be shared
● resources not entirely suitable for mass or other forms of group instruction can be used, such as computer-based training programs.

Individualized instruction has more delivery strategies than either of the other two methods. Most fall under the umbrella of open learning. Open learning is a flexible method of delivering learning materials where the learner has access to people, materials and equipment. The types of delivery method associated with individualized instruction are shown in Figure 7.4.

Other advantages of individualized instruction include:

● the many learner differences that can be taken into account
● the use of scarce resources
● the fact that learners are not required to attend regular classes; they can study at home or work
● the different forms of media that can be used
● the accommodation of different learning styles
● the allowance for cross-knowledge tuition
● the flexible enrolment procedures
● its cost-effective nature for a large number of users
● the changing role of the teacher to that of facilitator
● the learners having some choice over what, how and when they learn
● its effectiveness when the learners are isolated from the training institution
● it being active rather than passive learning.

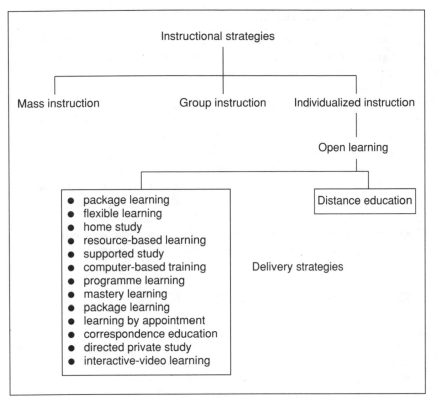

Figure 7.4 *Typical individualized instructional delivery strategies*

The disadvantages of individualized instruction

The disadvantages of individualized instruction include:

- low learner motivation that makes learning difficult
- the need for a relatively long lead time to develop course materials
- it not being suitable if the subject matter changes quickly
- the administration not being supportive of this type of instruction
- the teacher's role needing to change.

Many of these points could also be advantages. For example, changing the role of the teacher may be a disadvantage if they are resistant to change, but it could be an advantage if they are in favour of a role change.

Remember that individualized instruction needs more planning than mass or group based instruction to be effective.

Mixed mode instruction

Teachers often use several modes of instruction to achieve the various goals and objectives requires for the learning materials. For example, group-based instruction can be said to be a mixture of mass and individual instruction.

If you choose mass instruction as your instructional strategy and lectures as your delivery strategy, there is no reason why you shouldn't also use other methods of instruction. You may recognize the disadvantages of the lecture method, but still choose to use it for other reasons. However, to make the delivery of the learning materials even more effective, you can use elements of both group and individualized instruction at various stages throughout the learning event. This may overcome some of the disadvantages of mass instruction.

Using a number of different delivery methods is good for the learners as it accommodates their different learning styles.

SELECTING A METHOD OF INSTRUCTION

There are many factors you need take into account when selecting your delivery strategy and, once this choice has been made, there are still more choices that need to be considered.

Selecting the most appropriate method of instruction can be done by considering each of the following factors:

● number of learners
● type of content being delivered
● time you have to develop the course
● number of times you deliver the learning materials
● number of staff involved in delivery
● attitude of the staff
● number and type of support staff you have available
● type of educational environment you are teaching in
● physical design of your learning environment
● funds available to develop the materials
● administrative environment.

Each of the following cases illustrates how the various factors can influence the types of methods chosen.

Case study 1

You have been asked to deliver learning materials to a large number of learners. The event will be repeated many times. The learners are adults, their entry level skills are all different but your subject matter is relatively stable and will not change in the near future. You have some funds available and there is a long lead time to develop the materials. Many resources exist but some are not suitable for large groups as they use both video disk and computer-based training. Your colleagues, who will be teaching the course with you, are receptive to new ideas and appear to be innovative. The administration of the college is familiar with the traditional lecture and tutorial, but is a little hesitant about alternative delivery strategies.

How will you deliver the learning materials? You should start by asking yourselves a few relevant questions. Table 7.1 will guide you in this respect.

Given this discussion, you should have considered an individual instructional methodology. Individual instruction would appear the most suitable because:

- you have a large number of learners and the event has to be repeated many times
- the entry levels of the learners are different so self-pacing becomes an important consideration
- the subject matter is stable; any materials produced will be current for a long time
- you have some funds available which can be used for materials development
- some resources already exist
- your colleagues are supportive of change
- you have a range of audio visual and computer equipment
- the learners are all adults.

The administration is hesitant about the change from a traditional teaching environment, but you have enough positive factors to make it worth your while to try and convince them that change is for the better.

Case study 2

You have been given the task of developing learning materials for a group of tertiary students who do not have common entry-level skills.

Table 7.1   *Factors that affect the choice of delivery strategy*

Factor	Variable	Type of instructional strategy
Number of learners	large small	mass, individualized individualized, group
Type of learner	homogeneous heterogeneous	mass, group, individualized individualized, group
Type of content	skill-based process attitudinal knowledge	group, individualized mass, group, individualized group mass, group, individualized
Time to develop	long short	mass, group, individualized mass, group
Repeats of course	many few	mass, group, individualized mass, group
Number of staff	many few	group, individualized mass, group
Attitude of staff towards innovation	positive negative	group, individualized mass
Support staff available	many few	mass, group, individualized mass, group
Educational environment	traditional non-traditional	mass, group group, individualized
Design of learning environment	fixed changeable	mass mass, group, individualized
Funds available	large little	mass, group, individualized mass, group
Administrative environment	rigid flexible	mass mass, group, individualized

The materials will be delivered over a short period of time; there are no funds available for any developmental work; there are very few resources available; and the subject matter of the course is constantly changing. You will be the only one delivering the materials and the delivery will take place in a large lecture theatre. The topic is completely new to the learners and they have no previous background in the subject matter.

How would you deliver these materials? Here you might consider using mass instruction because:

- the materials have to be delivered over a short period of time and self-pacing does not seem possible
- there are no development funds available to develop learning materials
- there are few existing resources
- the subject matter is constantly changing which means the materials may not be of use in a future learning event
- the learners have had very little experience with the subject matter
- you will be delivering the materials in a large lecture theatre so the environment can not be changed.

Since the learners do not have a common entry level you may want to overcome this by using pre-reading assignments or preliminary lectures for those learners who need the added learning.

In this case mass instruction seems the most appropriate strategy because an overview of the topic is required and there is little opportunity for self-pacing because of the lack of funds for materials development.

Case study 3

You have to deliver skill-based materials to a group of secondary learners in the second half of term two. The learning objectives indicate that it is important that the learners interact with each other by working in groups to obtain the necessary skills using a problem-solving approach. There are very few learning resources for use with this topic.

How would you deliver these materials? In this case you may consider group instruction, as:

- the materials are skill-based and learners need to work together
- the materials must be delivered at a fixed time and place
- the learners are secondary students which could mean they are less able to work independently than adult learners
- there are few existing resources available and 'new' learning materials will have to be developed
- problem-solving skills are important in this case and small group work may be an effective way of achieving the objectives.

Learning materials always take a longer time to develop than you think, so plan for that right at the start of the project and don't be convinced to reduce the time frame to suit other needs.

Group instruction would appear to be the most appropriate strategy, especially since problem-solving skills have to be learned.

Given all of the preceding, however, there is no definitive answer to the correct selection of appropriate instructional strategies. You will have to make your judgement based on all the information you have available to you.

INSTRUCTIONAL MATERIALS

Whatever instructional strategy you have chosen to use, you will need various instructional materials to assist you to help the learners. Table 7.2 classifies instructional materials into print, audio visual and computer materials.

Table 7.2 *Classification of instructional materials*

Print	Audio visual	Computer
Chalkboard	Overhead transparencies	Computer presentation programs
Magnetic board	Radio broadcasts	Multimedia interactive systems
Posters	Television broadcasts	Computer-based training programs
Handouts	Tape and text	CD ROM programs
Self-instructional booklets	Slides	Interactive video
Assignments	Filmstrips	Video disk
Books	Audio tapes	
Displays	Audio discs	
Photographic prints	Slide-tape programs	
Models	Filmstrips with sound	
Real items	Video tapes	

Certain types of instructional materials are better suited to mass rather than group or individualized instruction, so the method of instruction you select has some effect on the type of instructional materials you use. Table 7.3 shows which instructional materials are more suitable as teaching aids for use by the teacher, which learning materials are for use by the learner, and those materials that could be used by both teacher and learner.

Table 7.3 *Classification of teaching aids and learning materials*

	Print	Audio visual	Computer
Teaching aids	Whiteboard	Overhead transparencies	Computer presentation programs
	Magnetic board	Radio broadcasts	
	Posters	Television broadcasts	
Learning materials	Handouts	Tape and text	Multimedia interactive systems
	Self-instructional booklets		Computer-based training programs
	Assignments		CD ROM programs
	Books		Interactive video
Teaching aids and learning materials	Displays	Slides	Video disks
	Photographic prints	Filmstrips	
	Models	Audio tapes	
	Real items	Audio discs	
		Slide-tape programs	
		Filmstrips with sound	
		Video tapes	

Instructional materials can be divided into two categories:

Use a variety of teaching aids rather than just one. Your learners will appreciate it.

- teaching aids
- learning materials

Teaching aids are those things used by teachers to assist them deliver the message to the learners. Teaching aids include whiteboards, flipcharts and overhead transparencies. Learning materials are those things the learners learn from and include self-instructional print materials, computer-based programs, interactive video disk and audio tapes. Some materials can be used with a number of various instructional strategies, for example, videos can be used as part of a lecture, or to stimulate a group discussion or they can be used individually by learners in a self-instructional mode.

Instructional materials should include both teaching aids and learning materials.

The classification of instructional materials into teaching aids and learning materials is a useful one. Some teaching aids are suitable for mass and group instruction, but rarely are they suitable for individual instruction. Similarly, various learning materials can be used in a lecture, but teachers would be more likely to use teaching aids such as the overhead projector to assist them deliver their lecture.

When you are selecting the appropriate instructional material you need to look at a number of factors. These are:

- the type of subject matter you are trying to deliver to the learners
- the type of instructional materials you are already using
- how available the materials are – can you buy the materials off the shelf, adapt commercial material for your own use, or do you have to produce the materials yourself?

CONCLUSION

At this stage of planning your learning materials, you have been faced with two questions: how do I deliver the learning materials and what instructional materials should I use? This chapter simplified your choice by giving you three instructional options. These are mass, group and individualized. Within each of these instructional options there are a number of choices you can make regarding the type of delivery strategy you can use.

The chapter also discussed the various types of instructional materials available to you. Typically these fall into two main categories:

teaching aids and learning materials. Some of these are more suitable for some types of instructional strategies than others.

Throughout this chapter you have seen that to limit yourself and your learners to only one type of instructional strategy and instructional material is not appropriate for the modern classroom. This approach to learning materials development must be changed if you are going to deliver learning materials effectively and give your learners the opportunity to learn.

Chapter 8
Can I Redesign The Materials I Have Now?

SUMMARY

Most of the discussion so far has centred around the design and development of 'new' learning materials. It could be, however, that you need to change or redevelop materials to make them appropriate for the project you are working on at present. It could be that the project you have been given involves redesign rather than the development of new materials. What does redesign mean? Does it mean that at the end of a number of years of use the materials are scrapped? What is scrapped, what is kept intact and what is revised? How is this done, how long will it take and who will do the job?

This chapter will describe a procedure for updating and revising existing learning materials to help you get the job completed in the most effective manner.

INTRODUCTION

Up to now this book has concentrated on the design and development of new learning materials. The need for course information has been described, as have profiles and the need for sound planning. However, if you followed the suggestions made in Chapter 2 of this book and searched out existing materials, you may be faced with the problem of trying to make these materials fit your new design scheme. Or somewhere a decision may have been made that existing learning materials just need updating. One of the issues you will have to face in redevelopment or updating is just how far you go. What should be revised, what needs redevelopment, what needs updating, what can be left as is and who best can do the job?

In many cases the revision of existing materials can be more difficult than the development of new materials because the required resources and the various criteria needed to help define the revisions are not in place and there is an unwillingness to put them in place. However, the redesign of learning materials should reflect an organized, systematic approach and must start with determining if the revision is warranted or viable.

GETTING THE PROCESS STARTED

Updating and redeveloping materials are not quite the same thing: updating could indicate mere tinkering with the materials (it is often more than that, however) and redevelopment suggests a tearing down to the bare bricks and rebuilding. For the purpose of this book, however, they will be treated as being the same thing because for the most part the procedures are the same, as is the end result: different, hopefully better, learning materials.

Most of the redevelopment decisions that you will have to make will revolve around questions such as, what should I do, how far can I go, and exactly where do I stop? Changes in learning materials can, like anything else, blossom into major productions that consume time, money and people, to the extent that budgets are often depleted for what, in the end, turns out to be something not much better than the original. Why does this happen? In most cases it can be traced back to the way that the redevelopment was conceived, a lack of resources being dedicated to the job and, most significantly, to the absence of a set of criteria to deal with the overall design. As an aside – to help overcome some of the tinkering problems typical with all course materials, you may wish to consider a regular learning materials update and content review by 'experts' in the field. This is a preventive maintenance approach to help resolve the problems associated with updating learning materials and which could help reduce the amount of materials that have to be scrapped.

To get the redesign process started, you should begin by reviewing the existing materials and determining just what it is that needs to be redeveloped. Go through the same procedure as outlined in Chapter 1 and ask yourself similar questions, with emphasis on the following:

The question that you should keep asking yourself is 'Where do I stop? At what point is the development finished?' When you answer the question stick to it!

- Who was the audience for these materials and is it the same audience now?
- What constraints such as time, financial and human, am I facing?
- Who will do what?
- Do these materials fit the objectives of my materials?
- How will this material fit with the instructional strategies I am considering?
- Does it fit the evaluation strategies I am considering?
- Should these learning materials be reformatted and if so how much work is that going to involve?
- What is the readability level of these materials and does it fit with my new materials?
- Do these materials fit into the new package?
- Are there any copyright problems?
- What are the costs of this redesign?

The answers to these and other questions should form the basis for developing your task overview sheets (see Chapter 1, section on course documentation).

A redevelopment project needs sound planning. Systematically go through all of the materials scheduled for redevelopment and list all of their problems. If the materials have a set of documentation similar to task overview forms and/or a CID or profile, review each of them and consider the changes needed as you understand them at the moment. If there is no documentation you should try to develop a CID and, using the goals and objectives as a guide – assuming of course that they are present in the learning materials – develop a profile. These documents should reflect the materials as you find them. If goals and objectives are not apparent, you are faced with reading all of the materials and trying to ascertain the goals and objectives. Not an easy task!

Once you have developed the CID and the profile, add those pages that describe the 'new' content and any changes needed and the treatment that can be given those materials. Remember that until you have validated the CID and completed a new profile, your additional pages are just guesswork, albeit intuitive guesswork.

It's at this point that you will have to make some difficult decisions. First you are going to have to decide if the materials as they are now will need a minor revision, a major revision or should be scrapped and new materials developed. Very few guidelines exist to help you here as your decisions will be based on the resources you have available and the project itself.

Planning is very important. Make sure that you spend enough time planning your redevelopment project.

It's possible that a significant amount of resources have already been expended on the project to date so, based on the decisions you have made regarding minor or major revisions or scrapping the material and starting again, you will need to meet with whoever assigned you to the project and present the CID with its additions and deletions. At this meeting it will be important that you first stress what changes are needed, and second that you would like to continue to the next stage of the project and complete two things. These are:

- developing a budget (make sure that you have enough resources to cover the validation of a new profile and the work involved in the comparison of the new profile with the existing one)
- conducting a small (emphasis here on small) amount of research to ensure that any materials you want to rebuild do not already exist in some other form.

Assuming that you are going to continue with the redesign up to the comparison of a new profile with the old, you should follow the procedures that have been described in Chapters 4 and 5 of this book. Meticulously plan and conduct your profile session, develop your sub-profile and validate all of your materials.

Once you have the new profile and sub-profile in place and validated, you will need to compare them again with the original documentation or with what you have reconstructed. As you make the comparison you can now make your final decision as to how extensive your redevelopment is going to be. Once your comparison is complete, outline your findings in a short report ready for review. You will not be able to complete any time line, milestones or products for the project until you have determined exactly what has to be done and who will carry it out. This will be based on the levels of treatment outlined in the next part of this chapter. The development of materials from those already existing is completed a little differently than the development of new materials. In this instance you should wait until you are sure what has to be done and, based on that information, develop your plans accordingly.

LEVELS OF TREATMENT

As noted at the beginning of this chapter, one of the major reasons for the failure of redevelopment projects is that exactly what will be carried out in order to complete the project is not determined.

Redevelopment is often carried out thinking that the materials development time can be reduced – don't get caught setting unrealistic time frames. Sometimes fixing can take longer than starting again!

Redevelopment requires that precise lists be developed to ensure that what needs to be done is done, no more and no less and all within a well-defined time line and budget.

You will find that keeping a redevelopment project on track can be more difficult than the development of new materials. Even with strict guidelines in place to describe what will be carried out at each level, it is often difficult to stop at a predetermined point, knowing that the materials could be just that little bit better if only you could carry on and do a little more.

In Chapter 1 it was suggested that for convenience learning materials could be broken into three categories; print, audio visual (AV) and computer-based. This chapter will continue with those same categories and review the tasks, expertise needed and the products that can be expected when you make both minor and major revisions to each of those kinds of learning materials.

MINOR REDESIGN OF PRINT-BASED LEARNING MATERIALS

Table 8.1 lists *minor* revisions to print-based learning materials that will result in a learner-centred design.

Use the table along with the guidelines suggested in Chapter 3 to help you determine the various tasks that need to be carried out, the expertise you may need to help you do the job and the product you should expect from that revision.

The table can also be used as a guide to help you determine a budget and time line and the place at which revisions should stop. The products of this minor revision might be an updated:

● (and validated) course information document
● teacher guidebook (it is assumed that these materials are teacher-independent)
● version of other learning materials
● version of the evaluation materials.

MINOR REDESIGN OF AV LEARNING MATERIALS

Print-based materials can have new materials inserted relatively easily into the existing ones; this is not as easy with AV materials. Prior to starting any project involving the revision of AV materials three questions have to be asked:

Table 8.1 *Minor revisions to print-based learning materials*

Type of materials to be revised	Task	Expertise required	Product
Print-based materials	*Information document* • develop or revise documentation	• Instructional designer	• CID
	Learner workbook • revise core content including: – summaries – embedded test items – other exercises, access devices – graphics – illustrations • revise hand-out design including: – charts – job aids – checklists • determine revised page and text formatting • proof-read and copy edit as necessary • obtain copyright clearance	• Subject matter experts • Writer(s) • Editor • Graphic artist • Information-entry person • Desktop publisher • Project manager (if the project is a large one)	• Learner workbook hand-outs, study and tutorial
	Evaluation • revise learner reaction sheet • revise teacher reaction sheet • redesign and revise assignments • revise tests • revise examinations	• Instructional designer • Subject matter experts	• Exams, tests and evaluation question-naires

- What is wrong with the materials as they are now?
- What is it going to cost to make these revisions?
- What is it going to cost to start again from scratch?

Of courses these are the same questions that you need to ask yourself about any print-based material revisions you are considering under-

Table 8.2 *Minor revisions to AV learning materials*

Type of materials to be revised	Task	Expertise required	Product
A/V-based learning materials	*Information document* ● revise documentation	● Instructional designer	● CID ● Story board
	Video tape ● update segments with new visuals ● update with new voice-over	● Subject matter experts ● Writer(s) ● Script writer ● Director ● Camera person ● Editor	● Updated video tape
	Evaluation ● revise learner reaction sheet	● Instructional designer ● Subject matter experts	● Evaluation question-naires

taking, but with AV materials they are particularly applicable. Unless and until each of these questions are fully answered you would be wise to not undertake any AV revisions.

Table 8.2 lists possible *minor* revisions that could be made to AV learning materials. Like the preceding table it can be used as a guide to help you determine a budget and time line and the place at which revisions should stop, as well as help you determine the various tasks that should be carried out, the expertise you may need to do the job and the product you should expect from that revision.

The products of this minor revision of AV materials could include:

● an updated voice-over on the video to change 'old' information
● new visuals or stills containing 'new' information
● new visuals to replace those showing out-of-date technology.

Remember that if more than 10 per cent of the video needs revision it is more cost-effective to scrap it and redevelop it from scratch.

MINOR REDESIGN OF COMPUTER-BASED LEARNING MATERIALS

Like the revision of AV materials, minor revisions to most computer-based materials are not generally considered to be a viable option. There is one exception, however, and that is the revision and/or updating of computer-managed learning (CML) test-item banks and course maps.

The three questions posed for the revision of AV materials also apply to computer-based materials. Table 8.3 lists possible *minor* revisions to computer-based learning materials. Again, use the table along with the guidelines suggested in Chapter 3 to help you determine the various tasks that you should carry out and the place at which revisions should stop.

The products of this minor revision could include new:

- CML test-item banks
- CML course maps
- option(s) placed at either the front or the end of a computer-assisted instruction (CAI) or multimedia presentation (those that would entail minimal re-keying or coding).

MAJOR REDESIGN OF PRINT-BASED LEARNING MATERIALS

Like the previous table showing minor revisions for print-based materials, Table 8.4 will help you determine the various tasks that you should carry out when print-based learning materials require major revision. As before, the table can be used to help you determine both a budget and time line and act as a guide to help determine the level at which revisions should stop. The products of this major revision are similar to those for the minor revision; however, here material formatting is more rigorous, the total appearance of the materials is standardized and substantial editing is carried out. A major emphasis is also placed on the need for and value of learner involvement and interaction with the materials.

The typical products of a major revision might be:

- a validated CID form
- a validated course profile and sub-profile
- a teacher guidebook

Table 8.3 *Minor revisions to computer-based learning materials*

Type of materials to be revised	Task	Expertise required	Product
Computer-based learning materials	*Information document* • revise new documentation	• Instructional designer	• CID
	CML test banks • redesign and revise assignments • revise tests • revise examinations	• Subject matter experts • Writer(s) • Editor • Graphic artist • Computer programmer	• CML test banks • CAI or multimedia presentation
	CAI materials • revise opening or closing screens		
	Evaluation • revise learner reaction sheet	• Instructional designer • Subject matter experts	• Evaluation questionnaires

- a learner workbook
- other learning materials
- evaluation materials, including reaction, in-course, tests and examination.

Table 8.4 *Major revisions to print-based learning materials*

Type of materials to be revised	Task	Expertise required	Product
Print-based materials	*Information document* • develop new documentation	• Instructional designer	• CID
	Course profile • develop new profile	• Materials designer and subject matter expert	• Profile

Teacher guide
- rewrite goals and objectives
- rewrite advanced organizers
- develop new lesson plans
- develop new in-course activities
- design new practice exercises
- standardize formatting
- conduct substantial editing
- obtain copyright clearance

- Subject matter experts
- Writer(s)
- Editor
- Graphic artist
- Information-entry person
- Desktop publisher

- Teacher workbook, hand-outs, study and tutorial materials

Learner workbook
- develop revised/new core content including:
  - summaries
  - embedded test items
  - other exercises, access devices
  - graphics
  - illustrations
- redesign handouts including:
  - charts
  - job aids
  - checklists
- determine page and text formatting
- proof-read and copy edit as necessary
- obtain copyright clearance

- Subject matter experts
- Writer(s)
- Editor
- Graphic artist
- Information-entry person
- Desktop publisher
- Project manager (if the project is a large one)

- Learner workbook hand-outs, study and tutorial materials

Evaluation
- develop new learner reaction sheet
- develop new teacher reaction sheet
- redesign and redevelop assignments
- develop new tests
- develop new examinations

- Instructional designer
- Subject matter experts

- Exams, tests and evaluation questionnaire

MAJOR REDESIGN OF AV AND COMPUTER-BASED LEARNING MATERIALS

The redesign of both AV and computer-based learning materials must start with a complete review of what already exists and if more than 10 per cent of the video needs redesigning or if new materials need to be inserted into the middle of a CAI or multimedia presentation, the materials should be scrapped and new ones developed. The expenditure of large amounts of resources often does not warrant the poor quality of the final product.

CONCLUSION

The answer to the question posed as the title of this chapter is yes! Yes, you can redesign learning materials but there are a number of factors that have to be considered to ensure the costs remain reasonable and the project is not a drain on resources. Redesign projects can be very large, and project management may be needed if, for example, a department within an educational institution decides to redesign of all its learning materials at the same time.

Chapter 2 in Book 2 of this series enters into a wider-ranging discussion of the various issues of materials redesign and provides you with a methodology to help you make rational decisions about the viability of redesign or scrapping the materials at hand.

Chapter 9

How Do I Assess The Learners *and* Evaluate The Learning Materials?

SUMMARY

The students passed, they were assessed, but what were the contributing factors? Could the learning materials have been better? What do you look at when it's the course that's being evaluated? This chapter is here to remind you that even during the planning stage, you must be clear about what you are to test, assess and examine regarding the learner's performance. It cannot be emphasized too strongly that even at this early stage you need to be clear about the use you are going to make of this information. At the same time, what information and tools are you going to use to collect information regarding the effectiveness of the course?

INTRODUCTION

What is a chapter on assessment and evaluation doing in a book on planning?

The first answer is simple. Frequently the tasks of assessment and evaluation and the tools used are last-minute considerations. Typically this leads to sub-standard assessment and poor evaluation practice. It is only natural, therefore, to include the considerations for assessment and evaluation processes 'up-front'.

The second answer has to do with the growing desire and need for effectiveness and efficiency in both education and training. To maintain credibility, in today's educational climate where there is a demand for quality assurance, you have to consider not only your learners and what they have achieved, but you must also take into account the effectiveness and efficiency of your actions and the learning taking place.

This raises the question about reporting the achievements of the learners to various groups involved in the assessment process. One group to be reported to are the learners themselves. In many settings there is a wider community who also need to be informed of the outcomes. This is particularly true at the pre-school and school levels where the wider community includes both parents and care-givers. At the education and training levels the wider community could include industry, family members and friends.

A further group that may need to receive reports are the people or institutions that provided the funds. This raises the issue of preparing and using budgets as a reporting tool; for many, this is a cause of concern. This chapter will provide you with guidelines and a model for preparing a budget.

The chapter is divided into four sections:

● Assessing learners
● Evaluating teaching and learning events
● Reporting the results
● Developing a budget

The discussion in each section is not exhaustive. The sections are included here to make sure that when you are at the planning stage you consider the various assessment tasks and evaluation strategies required.

This four-way division also indicates that there is more than a semantic distinction between assessing and evaluating. This confusion is often caused by using the terms as if they were interchangeable and they are not. Assessing a learner involves setting them a task and observing them carry it out. From an analysis of the information gathered as a result of the task being completed, it is possible to provide an evaluation of the status of the learner. This evaluation can be in the form of a report on the learner's status or a report on the actual learning materials.

ASSESSING LEARNERS: SOME GENERAL CONSIDERATIONS

Let us clarify some terms. In the educational community the terms 'test' and 'examination' are considered to be synonymous. The activities in tests and examinations are carried out by learners to provide you with information. In carrying out these activities, the learner is often required to perform in different ways. For example, a test may be conducted in a formal or informal setting, while an examination has a connotation of formality. Both could involve learners demonstrating their ability to use new knowledge of their ability to manipulate a piece of equipment.

The information collected as a result of these tests and examinations is collated as evidence to support an opinion about the learner. This information assists in the development of an evaluation of the learner. The two methodologies used in collecting this information are continual and final assessment. Continual assessment involves collecting information about a learner as an ongoing process. Final assessment is carried out at a pre-determined time or place, such as the end of term or semester, when a report on the progress of the learner is required.

Continual assessment is seen as a formative or ongoing assessment process that helps you develop an opinion, while final assessment is a summative procedure in that it provides you with details of the learner's progress to date. In many cases both formal and summative assessment are used as a barrier that the learner must pass through in order to proceed. The evaluation is also seen as a time when all the various data are collated and applied to all participants in the particular learning event.

If you are using continual assessment, the information you gather should contribute to the process of final assessment. However, using continual assessment is a process that allows the individual learner to progress in consultation with the assessor, who can authorize a learner to proceed through the course at their own pace.

During the planning stage there are many options open to you for developing an assessment scheme. These options will depend on the type of course that you are designing and what is appropriate for the presentation of the material, the activities learners undertake and the expected outcomes for the learners. For example, where the aim is to develop theoretical knowledge it will be more appropriate to have the learners carry out a task that challenges them to use the theory. Where the intended outcome for the learner is greater manipulative skills, then the task might include some practical demonstration components.

However, a scheme to assess learners will probably not rely on one assessment task or a set of similar tasks. For example, a learning event that is based on learning theoretical materials might include tests to determines if the theoretical considerations are known by the learner, as well as tasks to determine if these considerations can be applied in a given situation.

In developing any scheme of learner assessment you will also have to determine the standards that the learners will have to demonstrate. The source of these standards and the conditions which should apply when demonstrating the standards, should be your course information document and objectives statements regarding the intended learner outcomes. These statements could also provide you with information about the formal type of test(s), examination(s) or assessment task(s) you might use. If you are going to use informal methods, such as observation, then you will need to work those methods into the assessment proposal and provide a means of maintaining consistency between observations of the same learner and observations of different learners.

Tests and exams are tools to assist you in forming an assessment of the ability of the learner. A question-and-answer test will indicate if a learner has learned some facts. An essay question might indicate if a learner is able to use information in a reasoned manner. A project might indicate if a learner is able to bring together facts and information with the skills of production and presentation and exhibit appropriate attitudes through their production of the project.

The information you gain from these tools will enable you to reach some decisions about the learner and evaluate if the learner has:

Remember that testing and assessment are *not* the same thing.

- passed *(has passed what?)*
- reached a satisfactory standard *(what are the standards?)*
- areas of weakness that need to be improved *(what determines those weaknesses?)*

The point is that if you have not closely tied the assessment tools to the information you require, then you may find that the information you are getting is the 'wrong' information.

Table 9.1 shows a limited set of areas of knowledge, attitudes and skills that learners need. It relates these to possible test tools and an assessment task, and indicates a possible way of reporting the outcome to the learner.

Table 9.1 *Test tools and assessment tasks*

What do you want the learner to demonstrate?	Test tool (other tools could be used)	Outcome reported to learner
Knowledge: Facts and new information	Simple tests such as true or false, multiple choice and short answer	A quantity of 'correct' information
Knowledge: Application	Working through examples	Ability to apply new and known information
Knowledge: Synthesis	Essays and projects and learning contracts	Ability to use new information in other settings
Attitudes: Application	Observation of appropriate behaviour	Reinforce appropriate behaviour
Skills: Manipulation	Appropriate tool use	Correction of inappropriate tool use and reinforcing appropriate tool use
Skills: Application	Demonstrated use of a skill in a different setting	Reinforce the choice of tool or procedure made by the learner, perhaps question if the same choice would be appropriate in a different setting

While the chart is not exhaustive, it does indicate that the assessment task performed by learners need not be extensive and that it is what the learner does that provides the information you need. If anything, it reinforces the fact that in many learning settings it is good observation that gives the teachers the information they require to determine the development of the learner. The assessment tasks, as performed by the

Sometimes information on learners is easy to come by; however, this information is often overlooked.

learner, provide information that confirms the person has the 'already observed' capabilities.

One problem that must be constantly in the forefront of your mind is the need to treat all the learners equally. Remember, you cannot compare the results of assessment tasks that took place under different conditions.

In many cases easy information on the progress of learners will surface. In staff rooms, in common rooms, in teachers' offices, even in school corridors or anywhere that teachers congregate, at some stage learners will be discussed – either learners in general or particular learners. This discussion may lead to prejudicial views being formed about certain learners that may, in some cases, be negative. However, the discussion may be beneficial to the learner by providing you with second and third opinions about them. You will have to determine how, or if, you can use this information on the basis of your ethics and the ethics of your institution.

The reality of assessing learners and evaluating learning events

As part of the planning process there is a need for you to determine the role and value of gathering informal information and the relationship this should have with the formal information you collect. You, or you and the team involved in the materials planning process, will also have to consider how to incorporate informal feedback about the learning event. For example, how will you be able to document the difficulties learners had with a particular topic or a task within that topic that is not captured by the formal assessment tasks undertaken by the learner? This may be a reflection on the design and/or delivery of the materials and may have nothing to do with the abilities of the learners.

Planning to assess learners

When it comes to assessment tasks, simple things need simple tasks. Try to keep your learning materials as simple as possible.

The information collected on learner improvement needs to be uniform for each of the learners. It could include information about the observable changes in the learners' level of education training and knowledge, or simply what they have learned.

At a simple level you are asking for a comparison. What did the learner know before the course and how does this compare with what he or she knows after the event? There is an assumption here that you have information about the entry level knowledge or experience of the learner. This assumption needs to be tested. If the learner already knows the information, then the learning event at best reinforces what the learner is already capable of doing, but one would have to ask serious questions about designing a learning event to teach people material that they already know. To overcome this possibility you may have to devise a pre-test to determine the entry level of the learners. This information may well be part of your course information documentation and you should be able to find the minimum requirements for the learners listed there.

At a more complex level you are asking whether the learner can apply this new information or skill or attitude in the settings that they know, and you will have to devise tasks that provide you with this information. An assumption is that prior to the event the learners did not have the information or skills; this can be checked through the use of entry-level assessment tasks. The post-teaching assessment tasks should be designed to show that the new information or skill can be used by the learner in known or familiar settings.

At the most complex level you are asking whether the learner can apply this new information or skill or attitude in settings that are new to them: can the learners transfer known information to unknown situations in an appropriate manner? Remember that it is unreasonable to expect a learner to pre-test in an unknown situation, but you should expect a learner to be able to describe the application of their knowledge in a new but appropriate situation. This is a demonstration by the learner of their ability to recognize and apply new knowledge or skills.

There are also questions about the learner's change in behaviour. Is this going to play a role in your final reporting on the learner? If it is, how are you going to see that all learners are treated in the same way?

PLANNING TO EVALUATE TEACHING: SOME GENERAL CONSIDERATIONS

If you are planning to evaluate your teaching then you may use the results of learner assessment to reflect on your effectiveness in relation to the course. These 'results' of the learner are a 'quick' means of evaluating your teaching and the methods you used, but such an evaluation should include more than learner results.

At the same time, you do not want to add to your work burden, so some of the things you can do to provide you with the feedback you need should be incorporated into your work methods. If you are going to develop an evaluation scheme then you must be systematic.

The question you must consider is, how can my teaching be improved? This question means that you must determine how you can collect the relevant information. The issues involved include:

- the structure and presentation of the learning materials
- the use of various presentation tools
- your ability to foster interaction
- the tasks set for the learners.

You also need to consider the amount of flexibility you have to modify the learning materials once they are developed.

PLANNING AN EVALUATION OF A LEARNING EVENT: SOME GENERAL CONSIDERATIONS

Asking if the learners have achieved the objectives set for them is also asking what changes have taken place.

If you are setting up a scheme for evaluating the learning event then you may need to consider the following:

1. Did the learners achieve the objective(s)?

This question also suggests you consider what information you will need to enable you to comment on the structure of the materials, the methodologies and the appropriateness of assessment tasks.

2. Can the materials be improved?

Asking if the materials can be improved implies real improvement rather than minor modifications along the way.

This is a difficult question to answer because you are often basing your response on your experience with one group of learners; another group may react differently. The warning here is to be careful about the changes you consider based on one experience.

An introduction to the consideration of budget

You will also need to consider the cost of developing the learning materials. If you have a pre-development budget this will allow you to compare the costs of the development and delivery process; it really means that you will be able to compare your budget estimates with your actual expenditure. If your estimated costs are equal to your actual expenditure, then you came in on budget.

This discussion of budgeting leads to the need for reporting.

PLANNING YOUR REPORTING

If you are evaluating then you are also in the business of making reports. This in part has to do with information distribution, but it also has to do with accountability. You will need to consider the different audiences for reporting. The first is the learner, the second the community made up of parents and caregivers and the third is others interested and concerned with education and training, which could include the employers of adult learners and the potential employers of graduates from schools and universities. The other sector that needs to be reported to are the various funding bodies – institutions, government bodies, community organizations or all three!

There is also the issue of confidentiality. In our day-to-day activities as teachers we come across information relating to individual learners that may be confidential. Perhaps you are given the information as you assess the work of a particular learner. That the information may affect the assessment outcome for the learner is one thing, but you as a professional will have to determine your reaction to the information and its relevance in assessing the individual.

> Remember that there may be issues of confidentiality involved in reporting, so take care.

Reporting to the educational community

The way in which you make the information you gather available to the educational community will vary according to the needs of the various groups within that community. This also changes as the level of learning changes.

At school level the use of advisory meetings, report cards and parent/teacher interviews are the most common reporting activities. At the upper level of education, the posting of marks or grades and learner-initiated consultations are the main reporting means. There are of course tutor groups, but increasingly these are seen as content-oriented rather than for counselling. Reporting to the wider community at the upper levels of education is rarely done, but this is changing. Several countries have moved to a formal rating system of institutions of higher learning. This is an attempt to provide some quality information and is based on a range of criteria. Two examples are the level of research funding and student reactions to the courses they study. The attempt is to quantify academic excellence by a means other than the age of the ivy on the walls.

At the training level, reporting to the wider community is built-in; for example, the needs of 'masters' to know about their 'apprentices'. In companies where training needs are analysed and programmes developed and presented, the reporting on the outcomes for course participants may be widely distributed internally.

Planning the report on the learning event

There are four simple rules to follow when planning your report. The rule is to document the development process; this should be done using the CID. The second is to document any changes that occur during the development and delivery stages of the learning event. The third rule is to document the outcomes for the learners and the fourth is to act on suggestions for iterative changes.

Teachers make many changes on a small scale in the day-to-day activities involved in the teaching and learning process. However, even these changes need to be documented. This documentation will then provide the information to support ongoing change or an innovation. It may provide evidence for a wider change in the materials used.

To complete your evaluation of the learning materials other information that you need to collect is as follows. First collect what is easy to collect – collect what you can without resorting to things such as extensive surveys that add many extra hours to your day. Collect information that will indicate what the learner has learned if the learning promoted interest in the subject, content or activities and where the learners were interested in coming back for more.

Often some of these examples come easily to hand. These include collecting samples of learners' work, recording anecdotes of learner activity, their excitement and their moments of enlightenment. These simple indicators are often overlooked in favour of academic tools. However, while these informal means of data collection and analysis have a place, you need to consider whether they are relevant to your reporting needs. This will be dictated by your audience.

Reporting to funding agencies

Schools, colleges and universities cost money to build, maintain and run. The cost of maintaining an educational system at its current level could be under threat without evidence to make a case for that level of financial commitment. Reporting contributes to the justification for on-going financial support.

Funding agencies have always been important and in today's world the intrusion of the funding agency is reaching down to the level of the teacher. Most of the suggestions in this book will take you a long way towards reducing the fear or challenge of the funding agency, mainly because the learning events and their support materials, along with the budgets that go with them, are developed with a strong foundation of documentary support.

Planning the report format

The format that the reports might take will depend on your audience but could also be influenced by expectations raised by prior report formats and systems.

In pre-school and school settings the use of pro-forma report cards or booklets is widespread, although the headings on the cards and in these books vary. While this may cause some confusion for the outside observer there may be no problems for the people who receive the reports. The object of reporting is to provide information to the community of the learner about their status.

When reporting on a learning event, the extent of the report will vary. Sometimes a simple one-page report stating the purpose, followed by a brief description of activities and some short summary sentences of outcomes for the learners will provide all the information needed.

Reporting to funding agencies or about more substantial properties may require some detailed sections such as budget considerations and outcomes, all bound up with a one-page executive summary. The size of the project and the needs of the various stakeholders will dictate the size and format of the report.

PLANNING BUDGETS AND PLANNING BUDGET REPORTS

Just before you decide you don't need to read this section because your project is small and doesn't require more than petty cash items, perhaps you should read just a few more paragraphs.

Every time you make a change or modify learning materials you will need to be aware of various budget considerations. When planning your materials the main consideration will be the cost of your time. The first question you need to ask is how much of your time the development is going to take. If you find that the demands on your time are going to be extensive then you will have to determine the impact this could have on other calls on your time. In reality there are two costs: a real-time cost and a loss-of-time cost. The loss-of-time cost is made very real when you have to employ replacement staff to do your normal job while you undertake the project.

All projects have cost and therefore should have budgets.

If the project is of any size then real costs will need to be considered and these could range from stationery and phone calls to printing learning materials, shooting a video or developing a CD ROM. If the project is a large one, devoting time to budget considerations will be worthwhile. At the very least it will provide an economic rationale for your proposal.

Developing and keeping adequate documentation is important. For budgets there are usually three broad categories, described below.

Above-the-line costs

These are the costs of any resources and material that you 'buy in' for the project. A simple list would include:

- specialist staff to provide information on content
- learning materials
- copyright matters.

Below-the-line costs

These are the costs of in-house operations. In some large institutions this is not only your salary but also costs associated with someone monitoring the project and a proportion of the costs of in-house staff and material according to their contribution to the project.

Contingency at 10 per cent

In some cases this is called the 'mistake factor'. It is a sum of money set aside to cover costs that arise when unforeseen things occur.

By adding these three categories of costs together, you have a budget amount to help you plan, produce and deliver the learning materials and provide an evaluation.

You will also have an estimate of the cost of the project, which can be used for two purposes. The first is to justify the project, the second is to provide you with a tool for reporting on the project.

Once the various calculations have been completed, many educational projects tend to look very expensive. However, information from the CID on the life of the materials and the possible numbers of learners will help you justify the costs.

Setting out a budget for a project helps justify some of the costs and it also provides you with a reporting tool.

An example

(In the following example the term 'currency unit' is used rather than specific currencies.)

To develop a course costs 250,000 currency units. The materials are expected to last for up to five years. Spreading the cost over those five years means the material costs can be amortized, at 50,000 currency units per year. If there are only five learners in any one year it could indicate that it is a very costly learning event. If there are 50 learners per year it is less expensive. If there are 5,000 learners per year then your cost per learner is reduced even further.

All examples prove a rule. But this example contains an assumption that the learning materials will not need modification and therefore further cost inputs during the five year duration. The costs that you will or may need to consider are shown in Table 9.2.

Table 9.2 *Typical project costs*

	People	Items	Disputed areas
Above-the-line costs	Any 'freelance' people such as writers, consultants and media workers	Copyright production costs, post-production costs and support materials	Your time
Below-the-line costs	Your time; the time of the people you consult about the 'best way' of solving a problem	The infrastructure items and materials you use to assist you in the development of the project	The use of in-house facilities without cost recovery
Contingency	'Rescuers' or people you call in when the team doesn't deliver	The cost of re-doing material when the initial production is poor	The need for a contingency can be seen as an 'escape' for poor planning

A budget sheet might look something like the example in Table 9.3.

This list is not exhaustive and the line items will depend on the scope and scale of the project you are planning. You will also note that there are no contingency items. These should only come after you have budgeted for everything else.

It should also be noted that some items may appear in several places, such as administrative assistant(s) salary. You will therefore have to make sure that you are not budgeting for the same item twice. Also, items in the example may well be broken down into further parts.

With the information provided by a document such as this it is possible to compare the estimated costs and the final costs and determine efficiencies and outcomes for the learners on a cost basis.

Table 9.3   *Budget sheet considerations*

Project/Course	Cost estimates

Planning
  Cost of needs analysis
  associated cost with staff release
	Some of the line items
	Salaries of team members
	Consumables
	  Power
	  Phone
	  Postage
	  Stationery
	Rent
	Administrative Assistant(s)

Development
  Production of materials
  and support materials
  Staff development
	Print
	  Writers
	  Desktop publishing operators
	  Photographer
	Video [may need print people]
	  Director
	  Camera crew
	  Sound
	  Light
	  Cast
	  Location cost
	  Editing
	  Rights

Delivery
  Any staff and equipment needs
  and the costs of consumables
	Print
	  Paper and binding
	Video
	  Tape stock and duplication costs
	Distribution
	  Packaging
	  Post/courier
	Costs to administer/deliver

Evaluation
  Costs associated with developing
  an evaluation scheme and the
  materials to conduct the scheme
	Development of evaluation
	Printing and distribution
	Collating results
	Report writing

Then there are factors of skewing funds

With all the best intentions in the world some projects skew funds away from intended application. This places a cost burden on those activities. While this is a reality there are questions about how this can be budgeted.

When planning and developing large projects additional staff may have to be hired and this raises issues of taxation and pension entitlements, health insurance, workers' compensation and the like. Of course if you hire freelancers then some of these things are taken care of because the person is self-employed.

You might consider that taxes such as VAT and GST do not affect you, but tax laws vary from country to country and, in some countries, between the constituent states of countries. In some places goods for use in education are tax exempt, in other places they are not. If in doubt check it out.

The role of sponsorship

Sponsorship can be a source of funds but be very careful: budget input can lead to content control. Some sponsors, however, are keen to be associated with education and training and see their association as important, but prefer to have their input and their support recognized in a less intrusive way.

Final consideration on budget

There was a time when coming in under budget was seen as being foolish because the funding agency would take this into consideration the next time you applied for funds. The idea was to complete the project just over budget and spend the contingency fund on a new piece of equipment or expendables. The danger was that unspent money would be lost back into the system. However, with global budgeting being introduced into education and training in many countries and organizations, the responsibility of seeing projects through rests with managers and staff. Unspent money may be used elsewhere. But generally there are no funds to top up budgets.

CONCLUSION

Even in the early stages of planning a new development or a change in learning materials you will need to take into account the evaluation of those materials in terms of the outcomes for the learners and the materials themselves. This needs to be reported to several audiences within the educational community and to the funding body.

To assist you in this reporting process you need to document the process and consider budget reporting. Both of these will contribute to arguments supporting ongoing funding, further modifications and the efficiency of the process.

Chapter 10
Writing Test Items

SUMMARY

There are typically five reasons for testing or assessing learners. The first is to identify or diagnose their strengths and weaknesses. The second is to determine what has or has not been learned during instruction and, based on what is found, to prescribe something for the learner. The third reason is to assess individual performance in order to assign a grade, the fourth reason is to evaluate the quality of the unit of instruction and the final reason is to evaluate the learning materials.

This chapter reviews the development of both subjective and objective test items.

TESTING

Observations are always subjective. They reveal what is in the eye of the beholder, not what really exists. Teachers, however, must obtain information that is accurate and reflects what is actually happening, not what they would like to have happen. Tests are designed to replace a subjective measurement with objective measurement to the greatest degree possible because without the use of a well-designed and properly used test the teacher has no independent basis for assessing the behaviour of the learner. Tests allow you to monitor and evaluate what the learner has learned and diagnose strengths and/or weaknesses as they occur.

REASONS FOR USING TESTS

There are a number of reasons for using tests as a basis for judgement, some of which are as follows:

- to give objectivity to observation: measuring instruments are needed to help you record behaviour from a neutral vantage point
- to elicit behaviour under relatively controlled conditions: how can learner performance be judged when those judgements are limited by the many variables that operate in various situations? The testing situation must occur under conditions you can reasonably control
- to sample performances of which the learner is capable: to determine certain things about a person, you have to create a situation in which you can sample specific capabilities or tendencies
- to obtain performances and measure gains relevant to goals or standards: it is often not enough to know whether a person can do something; the question is how well learners can perform the skill after being instructed in it
- to apprehend the unseen or unseeable: the naked eye cannot see a person's attributes, values, or developmental levels; instruments are needed to reveal the unseen
- to detect the characteristics and components of behaviour: when given the opportunity to isolate behaviour or explore the performances of which a person is capable, you often need to obtain detailed information that might not be acquired during observation
- to predict future behaviour: since certain tests have been found to relate to future outcomes or events, it may be possible to predict future performance based on test outcomes
- to make data always available for feedback and decision making: testing provides data about outcomes such as the quality of learner performance and helps you make better instructional decisions.

WRITING TEST ITEMS

The most important aspect of a test is that its questions truly ask learners to show that they have learned what was taught them. The criterion for a good question should not be any one of the following.

- 'This one will make them think!'
- 'That sounds good.'

- 'I'll get 'em with this one!'
- 'I think we covered this anyway, they just *ought* to know it.'

As a general rule, every time you write a test question, ask yourself the following questions.

- 'What is this question *intended* to measure?'
- 'What is this question *really* measuring?'

When writing test items make sure that the items are directly linked to your learning objectives.

Testing is a controlled and objective procedure by which the performance of a learner can be sampled and evaluated against a standard.

The testing procedure makes data available for learner feedback to help you detect competence and determine the acquisition and possession of skills and knowledge. The success of any test, however, depends on how well the test is constructed, how well it is used, and how it is interpreted.

You cannot make valid judgements with a test that is imprecise or inaccurate. The worth of a test is measured in terms of its validity and reliability. Validity means that the test measures what it is supposed to measure. To establish validity you should have some independent way of assessing the property that the test is supposed to measure. Reliability refers to the test's consistency. Does the test measure the same thing each time it is used? Whatever a test measures it must provide as error free an estimate of the property to be measured as is possible.

ESSAY AND SHORT ANSWER/COMPLETION QUESTIONS

A test question either asks learners to provide an answer, or it asks them to choose an answer from a list of possibilities. Essay questions and short answer or completion questions are the two forms that ask the learner to supply the answer. Matching exercises, true/false and multiple-choice questions are the forms used for asking the learner to select an answer.

The essay question asks the learner to supply an answer. You can ask the question in such a way that the learner is given complete freedom to express his or her ideas, for example, 'Discuss changing attitudes toward care of the aged'.

More commonly, however, the essay question is asked in a way that restricts the learner's response in some way. Here, you may want to limit the content area or the manner in which the learner is to respond, for example:

A well written test item is more 'fun' to mark!

In no more than three pages, list changes in attitude by health professionals in the last 25 years toward the care of the aged in terms of home care. To what events or research developments do you attribute these changes in attitude?

Advantages

There are some advantages to using the essay question.

- It is the best way you can assess a learner's writing ability.
- It is the only type of question that can measure verbal self-expression.
- It is the best way for you to assess a learner's ability to create, organize, synthesize, and evaluate ideas.
- The essay question can measure a learner's global attack on a problem as well as their problem-solving skills.
- You can use it to measure attitudes, values and opinions.
- It can be used effectively when an objective calls for the ability to *recall* rather than *recognize* information.
- Essay questions are *relatively* easy to construct as compared to objective questions.
- Learners cannot guess the 'right answer'.
- Essay questions are practical for use with small groups.
- Essay tests can be good learning experiences.

Allow learners to review the test and change their answers if necessary. Reviews do not affect the outcome of a test.

Disadvantages

Unfortunately, the disadvantages of essay items outweigh the advantages. These disadvantages centre around the basic issues of test design – validity and reliability.

- Because of their length, essay questions can sample only a limited number of your course objectives.
- Essay items are not the best way for you to measure simple comprehension, rote memory of facts, or to answer 'who, what, where, when' questions.
- Scoring essay questions is extremely difficult, time-consuming and unreliable.
- Essay tests favour the verbally adept learner.
- Bluffing is common and not always easy to detect.

Design

The following guidelines will help you maximize the effectiveness of the essay type question.

- Learners have the right to know exactly what is expected of them, so the questions must be made as clear and unambiguous as possible.
- Don't give the learners a choice of questions, since this makes the scoring very unreliable.
- Use a relatively large number of brief-answer (half-page) questions in order to sample the objectives adequately.
- Whenever possible, present a novel situation.

Scoring

Two major methods can be used to increase the reliability and fairness of scoring an essay test; these are the analytical and rating methods.

The analytical method

1. Before giving the test, construct an ideal answer to each question – break each question down into its different parts and identify the major points that should be covered by the learners' answers.
2. Read the learners' responses and give scores for points covered, based on a rating scale.

The rating method

1. Before giving the test, construct an ideal answer to each question.
2. Read the learner's answer and classify it into one of three to five categories, such as poor, average, good.
3. Read and classify the responses once or twice and average the ratings.

After you have written the test, review it for face validity (how it looks to the learner).

Regardless of the method of scoring, there are several things you can do to increase the reliability of your scoring.

- Before actually scoring the tests, pick a few answers at random to see how they compare to the ideal answer.
- Grade all papers anonymously.
- Read all the learners' responses to one question at the same time before moving on to the next question.

- Score all answers to one question without interruption so that all learners are exposed to a consistent mood or frame of mind.
- Provide comments and correct the learners' errors so they have a basis for understanding their mistakes.
- Evaluate the mechanics of expression, which should be scored separately from the content.
- Determine a policy for how to score irrelevant or illegible responses.

An essay question can be written as a short answer when it contains only one central idea and can be answered in one or two sentences. Items that require your learners to supply definitions or short explanations of concepts and relationships fall into this category.

Answers to extended-answer essay questions can be from half a page to several pages in length. You can use this type of question to measure a learner's ability to deal with complex relationships, comparisons and evaluations.

You should indicate the desired length of the response in the question. The use of the phrase 'in one or two sentences' or 'briefly' as restrictive terms do not help the learner or you as they fail to specify your intent. The question should have limits such as time, 'this question should take you no more than ten minutes' or worth, 'this question is worth 10 marks.' You can also place other restrictions on the learner by limiting the space allowed for the answer. On take-home examinations limits such as 'Your response must be limited to no more than three double-spaced typewritten pages' or 'In 500 words or less ...' should be used to help the learner answer the question to the best of their ability.

SHORT ANSWER/COMPLETION QUESTIONS

After you have written the test, review it for content validity (do the items test appropriate knowledge and skills?)

The second type of question that asks the learner to provide the answer is the short answer or completion question. The completion item can take one of three forms: the question format, the incomplete sentence format, or the association format. The best method is the question format where you present the information as a question and ask for specific, limited information.

The incomplete sentence format should be used sparingly because items written in this format are often obvious or ambiguous. The association form consists of an introductory statement used to establish a frame of reference and a set of related words to which the learner is to respond. This type of item is similar to the matching type item.

Advantages

The advantages to using a short answer/completion question are:

- it is one of the easiest types of questions to construct
- it can be used to measure simple learning, such as recall of information
- learners cannot guess the answer or rely on partial knowledge
- reliability and validity are increased (as compared to essay items) because more objectives can be tested
- the short answer/completion question is the best way to check certain mathematical skills. For example, when you are testing computation skills or the ability follow a formula, the learner cannot solve the problem by working backwards from a given solution.

Disadvantages

As with the essay question, the short answer/completion question is characterized more by its disadvantages.

- They are very difficult and tedious to score. You frequently have to make decisions about partial answers or about unexpected but correct (or partially correct) answers that result from a different interpretation of the question. Poor handwriting can also interfere with the scoring.
- The scope of information that this type of question can adequately test is limited to that which can be stated in a single word, symbol or phrase.
- It is almost impossible to design short answer/completion questions that evaluate complex learning, such as the ability to analyse.

Design

- The question should be written so that there is only one short definite correct answer. Learners, however, will always come up with unexpected but true responses. For example:

Poor: Beethoven was a ...

Better: What was Beethoven's nationality?
_____ (German)

Some of the answers you could expect from your learners might include 'composer, musician, German, great man'.

Consider the answers you might get to the following question:

A_____ weighs less than a kilogram.

A better way to write it might be:

What unit of measurement is exactly 1/1000 of a kilogram?
_____ (Gramme)

In some items the use of the article 'an' indicates that the correct response must start with a vowel and therefore there are a number of technically correct answers.

- Specify precisely the terms in which your learners should answer.
- Do not remove statements verbatim from your learning materials.
- Avoid giving clues that give the answer away or make it easier to guess.
- Make each item independent of all the others.
- Omit only significant words, but be careful not to mutilate the statement. For example:

  Poor: Bach created _____ in every _____ form except _____
  Better: Bach created masterpieces in every baroque form except _____('Opera')

- Whenever possible, put the blank at the end of the statement.

Scoring

Make sure that your test is 'content balanced' and matches your learner profile.

- List all the possible acceptable answers on the answer key before grading the tests and give equal credit for each. Let your learners know if spelling will be marked.
- Give one point per blank, not per question.
- Put all the blanks for the answers in a column along the edge of the page. This will make scoring faster and easier.

TRUE/FALSE, MATCHING AND MULTIPLE-CHOICE QUESTIONS

The alternative family of questions consists of true/false, matching and multiple-choice questions, otherwise known as objective questions. These questions present learners with a list of possible answers. The learner chooses the answers they think are correct.

OBJECTIVE QUESTIONS

Advantages

There are several important advantages to objective questions.

- You can use them to test learning at any level.
- They are easy to score, either by non-professionals or by machine.
- They are efficient. Compared to essay or short-answer tests, it takes less time to answer more questions. This factor increases the test's reliability and validity because the test can cover more content at greater depth. The result is a more complete picture of what has been learned.
- Learners cannot bluff their way through an objective test.

Disadvantages

There are some disadvantages of objective testing, some of which are insurmountable.

- They are more difficult and time-consuming to design than essay or short answer tests.
- They can encourage rote learning.
- It is difficult to design questions which test complex learning.
- Learners often resort to guessing.

Design

Whichever form of objective question you decide to write, there are some general guidelines to follow that apply to all objective questions.

- Learners must be given a fair chance to show what they have learned. Help them out by asking clear, uncomplicated questions. This can be done by using words that are precise and by avoiding complex or awkward word arrangements. Keep the reading level low in relation to the learners you are testing.

  - Avoid using a particular response pattern, such as TFTTFT or babcbd.
  - Avoid making the correct answers consistently longer (or shorter) than the incorrect answers.
  - Avoid using grammar that provides clues to the answer. For example:

Determine the length of your test by reviewing the materials you are teaching and specifying the percentage of items selected from each category.

A newt is an example of a(n)
a fish
b amphibian
c reptile
d bird

To which group of vertebrates does the newt belong?
a fish
b amphibians
c reptiles
d birds

– Be sure each item is independent of all the others. A common error is to include a question that provides a clue to another question later in the test. For example:

An acid spill should be cleaned up using
a a caustic neutralizer
b an acid neutralizer
c water
d ptyalin

A neutralizer should be used to clean up
a a caustic spill
b a flammable spill
c any type of spill in the lab
d an acid spill

The second question helps provide the answer to the first question. This occurs most often when questions are written at different times and placed in different parts of the test.

● If a question is written based on an authority's views that are likely to be controversial or debatable, cite the authority. For example:

There is a direct link between smoking and impotence in men.
True   False

A better way of writing the question would be as follows:

According to the American Society of Addiction Medicine there is a direct link between smoking and impotence in men.
True   False

- When designing the whole test, group each type of question together so learners won't have to waste time adjusting to different thinking patterns. Write clear, explicit directions. Provide a method for learners to mark their responses that is both easy for them to use and easy for you to score.

TRUE/FALSE QUESTIONS

The true/false test consists of a statement with some way for the learner to register agreement or disagreement.

After you have written your test items put them away for a few weeks then try them out. Consider both face and content validity as you take your test.

Advantages

- The test can be scored by someone unqualified in the subject area.
- The scoring is completely objective.
- The test can be administered quickly.
- The structure of the item is less complex than other selection type items.
- The statement need not include instructions on how to respond.
- It is less difficult to write and refine true/false items.

Disadvantages

- There is a possibility of a learner getting half of the items correct by chance.
- The test is of little value in determining gaps in the learner's knowledge.
- Items often do not discriminate well between those receiving the highest test scores and those receiving the lowest scores.
- The true/false test is less reliable than other forms of objective tests of equal length.
- It is often difficult to develop items that can be answered absolutely true or false.
- The true/false item is not appropriate for measuring complex understanding.

Keep all the questions on the same page. Do not put a page break in the middle of a question.

Design

When designing a true/false test consider the limitations of the test format and select only those items from objectives that lend themselves to measurement with items of this type. Those objectives that do not lend themselves to measurement using the true/false item should be measured using other item types. By following this simple rule you will create a more valid test.

Usually the instructions for registering agreement or disagreement for the true/false test are part of the test directions appearing in a separate paragraph, however, instructions specific to a cluster of true/false items may also appear in the test as an introductory statement for the item cluster. For example:

> The following sentences may or may not contain grammatical errors. If the sentence is grammatically correct mark out the T. If the sentence is not grammatically correct mark out the F.
>
> T   F   I heard you was at the Marina.
>
> T   F   He didn't plan to study education at the university.
>
> T   F   Are you calling us?
>
> T   F   The back tyres had worn out.
>
> T   F   This mobile phone works good.

You can also write a true/false item in such a way that the learner is not only asked for a true or false answer, but is also asked to identify the incorrect element in the sentence and correct it. The disadvantage to this is that the item can often be changed to a true statement in a number of different ways and you must take care to ensure that the item is not ambiguous.

Also when the learner is asked to answer an item of this type the speed of responding is reduced and fewer items can be answered during an exam time limit. It also takes longer to mark this kind of item as it cannot be done using a scoring machine.

MATCHING QUESTIONS

Another member of the objective test question family is the matching exercise, which is in fact a specialized form of multiple choice item. Here two parallel columns of information are presented and the learner is asked to match each word, number or symbol in one column with a word, sentence or phrase in the other column. The items the learner is trying to match are called *premises* (the left-hand column). The items the learner chooses from are called the *alternates*. The directions usually state the basis on which matches are to be made.

There are some common variations in the design of matching exercises. For example, the question may have an unequal number of premises and alternates, which makes answering more difficult. Another variation is to provide the option of using responses once, more than once or not at all.

Advantages

- They are relatively easy to construct and score.
- They are compact and efficient and a large amount of related material can be tested in a short period of time and space.
- It is not as easy for learners to guess as it is with true/false questions.

Disadvantages

There are some disadvantages to using matching exercises in your tests.

- They encourage rote memorization on the learner's part.
- Their use is limited to testing homogeneous material.
- It is difficult to design exercises that test complex thinking and learning.

Design

The following guidelines should be followed when you are designing matching type items.

- Use only logically related material in a single exercise. Each response should be a plausible answer for each premise.
- Avoid using an equal number of responses and premises. This way the learner's answers are not the result of a process of elimination.
- The directions should tell the learners the basis on which they are to make a match. The directions should also state whether a response can be used once, more than once or not at all.
- Matching exercises are best used with homogeneous subject matter to test learners' ability to match items, definitions, dates, events, cause and effects, and other matters involving simple relationships.

- Arrange the exercise so the learner can answer the question efficiently.
  - Arrange the responses in a logical order, such as alphabetical or numerical.
  - Place the entire question on one page so the learner doesn't waste time flipping back and forth between pages.
  - Limit the number of premises to no more than ten.
  - Create more alternates than premises.

MULTIPLE-CHOICE QUESTIONS

The most versatile type of objective question is the multiple-choice question. In its standard format, it consists of a stem, which presents the problem, and a list of possible answers called distractors whose function is to distract those learners who are unsure of the correct answer. The learner selects the one correct or best answer from this list.

There are many variations of this standard multiple/choice question. Some of the most common include the following:

- Reverse multiple-choice, where all but one of the suggested answers are correct.
- Combined response, where in addition to the stem, a list of options is presented. The suggested answers are different combinations of these options, for example:

Indicate which of the following statement(s) are **correct**:

Statement 1	All chemicals can be stored in any cabinet or shelf
Statement 2	Chemicals should be stored higher than four feet off the ground
Statement 3	Chemicals should be stored according to their compatibility with other chemicals
Statement 4	Chemicals should be stored according to the size of the container

a 1, 2   b 3, 4

c 2, 3   d 1, 4

- Analogy, in which three parts of an analogy are given and the learner chooses the fourth part from the suggested solutions.

The Anopheles mosquito is to malaria as the Aedes mosquito is to

a   ebola
b   Nile river blindness
c   dengue fever
d   sleeping sickness

Advantages

There are many advantages to using the multiple-choice question.

- It is possible to design high-quality items that test even very complex learning.
- Multiple-choice questions can be used to test material that is neither homogeneous nor clear cut.
- The multiple-choice question is usually less ambiguous or confusing than either true/false or matching questions.
- Multiple-choice questions can provide valuable diagnostic information. By examining a learner's incorrect answers, you can find clues about the nature of his or her misunderstandings.
- Multiple-choice questions avoid the problem of response sets. That is, learners don't have a tendency to prefer a particular response when they don't know the correct answer.
- The effects of guessing are small compared to true/false questions.

Disadvantages

Even though multiple-choice questions are the most highly recommended type of test question, there are some drawbacks to using them.

- Of all the types of test questions, they are the most difficult and time-consuming questions to design well, partly because of the difficulty of writing effective distractors.
- Multiple-choice questions take more time to answer than the other objective questions, so less material can be tested.
- Learners with low reading ability or limited experience taking tests have more difficulty answering multiple-choice questions.

Design

Consider the following guidelines when designing multiple-choice tests.

- Use clear, unambiguous, precise language. The easiest way to write a clear item is to ask a direct question rather than present an incomplete statement as the stem.
- If an incomplete statement is used, include as much information in the stem as possible. Make sure the solutions come at the end of the statement, not at the beginning or in the middle. This will save reading time as well as printing space. For example:

> Poor: What did Margaret Thatcher do after she stepped down as head of the British Conservative Party?
>   a   wrote her memoirs
>   b   formed a consulting company
>   c   became a TV talk show host

> Better: Margaret Thatcher, after she stepped down as head of the British Conservative Party
>   **a**   wrote her memoirs
>   b   formed a consulting company
>   c   became a TV talk show host.

- Do not make the correct answer consistently different from the distractors. For example, making the answer longer, more detailed, or following a systematic pattern (a,b,d,a,b,d).
- Try to eliminate verbal associations between the stem and distractors. For example:

> Poor: The price the buyer pays for goods is called the:
>   a   cost
>   b   selling price
>   c   gross profit
>   d   net profit

> Better: The amount the buyer pays for goods is called the:
>   a   cost
>   **b**   selling price
>   c   gross profit
>   d   net profit

● Consider overlapping distractors.

    Which of the following play a role in digestion?

    1   tonsils
    2   pancreas
    3   appendix
    4   large intestine

    a 1,2,4   c 2,3,4
    b 2 only   d 2,4

Since 2 is included in each of the options, the learner will always select it. You have not learned whether he or she knows that the pancreas is involved in the digestive process.

    This is another example of overlapping distractors.

    In the story of 'Georgie Grows Up', Georgie was a young:

    a boy   c son
    b lad   d girl

If the answer to this question is not 'girl', the learner will be right no matter which of the other three options is chosen.

● State questions and options positively. The only time you should use a negatively stated item is when it is critical to know what *not* to do. Use bold for 'not' so the learners see it.

    In an unwitnessed cardiac arrest with no breathing or pulse, the rescuer should **not**:

    a give the precordial thump
    b maintain a 15.2 ratio
    c. open up the airway
    d give four initial quick breaths.

● Use 'none of the above' and 'all of the above' sparingly. Use 'none of the above' as an option only when it is necessary for the learner to know that all the distractors are wrong.

    The first president of Singapore was:

    a George Yeo
    b Lee Kuan Yew
    c Ong Teng Chong
    d none of the above

Since 'D' is the correct answer, you still have not tested whether the learner knows who was the first president. Using 'all of the above' encourages guessing. The combined response question, discussed earlier, avoids the problems of 'all of the above'.

THE INTERPRETATIVE EXERCISE

The interpretative exercise is a unique test item that often combines many types of objective questions. An interpretative exercise presents some introductory material to the learner, such as charts, graphs or a short reading. The test consists of a series of questions that ask the learner to interpret the material. The questions may be of the true/false, matching or multiple-choice variety, or some variation.

Advantages

- It can measure more complex learning than most of the other questions. Some examples of the types of learning it can test include measuring a learner's ability to:
  - apply principles
  - identify cause–effect relationships
  - identify unstated assumptions
  - assess the relevance of an argument or adequacy of a procedure.
- They are an effective way of simulating a natural situation.
- They are challenging and many learners enjoy them.

Disadvantages

- They are very difficult items to design.
- They often place a heavy demand on a learner's reading skills.

Design

- Choose the introductory material carefully. It should be brief, novel, creative and on a non-demanding reading level.
- The questions should be related only to the introductory material.
- Keep the number of questions proportional to the length of the introductory material.

See Figure 10.1 for an example.

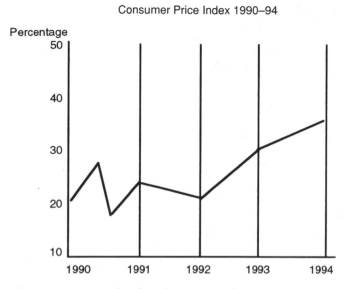

Figure 10.1 *An example of an interpretative exercise*

Answer the questions based only on the information given in the graph. Check your answer sheet by marking space if the:

a   item is definitely true
b   item is probably true
c   information given is not sufficient to indicate any degree of truth or falsity in the item
d   item is probably false
e   item is definitely false

SUMMARY

Writing test items is a difficult task at best. However, knowing some of the basic rules and understanding where and how various types of test items can and should be used will enable you to construct better tests for your learners. It is important to remember that the form of a test gives no certain indication of the ability tested and that as you develop your test you must seek to make sure your measurements are as objective as possible and an outline or profile of topics the learner is expected to achieve should always be the basis for your test items. See Table 10.1 for a summary of the types of test items covered in this chapter.

Table 10.1 *Summary*

Item type	Best used to assess	Not best choice for assessing
Essay items	Creative thinking Global, integrative thinking Problem-solving Writing ability Self-expression Organizational skills	Simple recall (who, what, when, where)
Short answer/ completion items	Simple recall only Knowledge of terminology, formulas, symbols and/or calculations	Any complex thinking Recall of information that cannot be stated in words, symbols or formulas
Objective items (general)	Any simple and complex learning depending on type	Creative, original thinking Writing ability and self-expression
Multiple-choice items	Simple and complex learning	–
True/false items	Knowledge of cause and effect Attitudes, superstitions and misconceptions Information with definitely correct answers	Complex learning and thinking
Matching items	Associations and relationships within homogenous material Definitions	Complex learning
Interpretative items	Applying knowledge to new situations Evaluative thinking skills	Simple knowledge

Chapter 11
Copyright

SUMMARY

This chapter discusses some of the issues you need to consider regarding copyright. What can and can't be copied from books and, in an on-line environment, what are some of the issues with respect to the World Wide Web and downloading materials for use in your on-line classroom or simply linking your learners to other Web pages?

INTRODUCTION

Typically, four questions are asked in reference to copyright. These are as follows:

1. Can I photocopy a newspaper article or cartoon or a part of a book without first obtaining copyright?
2. Because I use something for educational purposes does that mean that I do not have to obtain copyright?
3. Can I download materials from the Web for use in my learning materials?
4. What are the penalties if I infringe copyright?

The answer to the first question is simple – no, you cannot photocopy a newspaper article, a cartoon or part of a book without first obtaining permission!

The answer to the second question is somewhat more complex. In most instances copyright permission must be obtained even if your materials are being used for educational purposes. The only exception is if you make a single copy of a portion of the work (up to approximately 10 per cent) for your private study, research, critique or criticism. If you copy an article or portion of a book for use in your learning event it is not considered private study.

As for the third question, in a word the answer is no! This is explained later in this chapter. As for the final question, the penalties you face for copyright infringement range from personal embarrassment to substantial fines and even imprisonment. Most of you do not have to worry about the most drastic penalty, since it applies mainly to copiers of patented industrial processes or major computer software 'pirates'.

However, many countries are coming down hard on copyright violations since the signing of the Berne copyright convention in 1989.

COPYRIGHT DEFINED

Copyright is someone's ownership of intellectual property they created. Don't abuse the right of ownership!

Copyright is a person's ownership of the intellectual property he or she has created. A copyright does not have to be registered, but should be if the person wants to prove ownership. The copyrighted material must be in tangible form, that is, it must be written down on paper or in a computer file or Web page, taped, painted, or otherwise expressed so that it can be seen, heard or touched.

COPYRIGHT INFRINGEMENT

If you are employed as a lecturer, teacher or trainer in an educational institution or organization and as part of your job you have to design and develop course materials, the copyright is owned by that institution or organization unless your contract specifically states otherwise.

One way that you can avoid copyright problems is to use only those materials written by authors who have been dead 50 years or longer. This may be easy with some topics but it would be very difficult for those who are expected to be familiar with, write about and develop learning materials regarding the latest trends and theories in wafer fabrication, for example.

Educational institutions and universities in countries such as Australia, Britain, Canada and America are attempting to have the copyright laws modified to allow some reproductions for use in the classroom, but so far they have had only limited success. In some countries, copyright collectives have been formed to sell educational institutions broad licences to copy materials produced by their members, but to date, the number of collectives and the authors they represent is limited. In other instances legal firms have been assigned the job of collecting copyright payments on behalf of authors or the copyright owners.

It is important that you understand that copyright infringement applies regardless of the technique used to copy the material or the amount being copied. On many photocopying machines in educational institutions and organizations throughout the world an extract from the Copyright Act is placed that describes a 'reasonable portion' of materials. Reasonable portion is defined as applying not only to the quantity of material, but also its quality. For example, several paragraphs of a text could be copied, totalling about 100 words, from a 200 page book without infringement problems, but a short poem or a piece of music would be another matter, in that it would be difficult to copy only a small part.

A short poem or piece of music that is part of a large collection is a work in its own right and therefore the reasonable portion concept would not apply.

The use of the computer has added an interesting dimension to the issue of copyright. For example as a person 'surfs' the net the browser makes copies of Web pages and places those pages into temporary files. These files are accessible and downloadable to the user simply by copying them from temporary storage to the computer's internal drive for permanent storage. These pages can also be copied, perhaps inadvertently, onto back-up tapes for archival storage. To date the law is unclear as to how this affects the copyright laws.

FAIR USE

Fair use or fair dealing exists to stop copyright laws from preventing or stifling criticism or critique of a book, film or article, etc. Fair use means that you can make limited use of the work without permission. In the case of the Web, however, again the law is unclear. The best advice here is to get permission first.

COPYRIGHT ISSUES

Most works created after 1 April 1989 are copyrighted and protected by law. Most major countries follow the Berne copyright convention so you have to assume that the work is copyrighted unless you know otherwise. You should not assume that because you have not charged a fee to others for materials that you have copied without permission, that you have not violated copyright; you have, charging a fee makes no difference to the illegality of the act, except when you get to court and the judge increases the fine accordingly.

Never assume that a work is in the public domain. Unless the owner has explicitly told you that it is, and you have the paper to prove it, the work is not in the public domain. As a final point, you should also understand that when the work is in the public domain, the owner of that work has abandoned all rights to that work and then, and only then, are you legally able to use that material without permission.

COPYRIGHT AND THE WORLD WIDE WEB

As a creative work a Web page is not much different from a magazine or book page, except that a Web page may contain graphics along with both audio and video files. As a whole product the page is protected, but the problem lies in the browser used to display the page to the user. Different browsers display the same page in different ways and browsers can be modified by the user to display pages differently. Does this mean that copyright has been violated, or that you can copy these disparate elements for their own use because they no longer make up what was intended in the original design? No! As long as the arrangement you see on your screen is original, then the design of the page and the elements on that page are protected by copyright.

You also have to be careful about clip art or other similar materials you may have gathered to use on your Web site. Yes, you have paid for the use of the graphic but some art can't be used in or on a fee paying site. Make sure that you read the fine print in the copyright statement.

As educators and trainers some of you may have already, or may be considering developing on-line learning materials as a means of delivering a learning event to your learners. As is common in many on-line learning environments, learners are often directed or linked to other Web sites. This is fine, but a word of warning: at present directing and/or linking your learners to other Web sites is a very grey area with respect to copyright. As far as the copyright law is concerned a

Uniform Resource Locator or URL is a fact just like a street address is not copyrightable, but a list, particularly an alphabetized list of URLs, may be subject to copyright if it is deemed to contain some originality.

If, for example, a person has spent many hours reviewing Web sites, listing them and creating an alphabetized link list, that list is considered to be a creation and, therefore, copyrightable. If you then copy that list to your learning materials it probably is a copyright violation. However, if you were to take several links from the list and provide them to your learners it probably would not be a violation of copyright.

Putting direct links from your learning materials to other Web sites may also cause problems. At present, it has been noted by copyright lawyers that there is something called a doctrine of implied public access on the Web. If a Web site has been created and is available to the general public, the creator or owner of the site has given implied permission to others to link to their site, and they in turn are able to link to other Web sites. This implied permission is fine and works up to a point, but only if the Web site being linked is reputable and the so-called 'assets of your learning materials' are not diminished by such an association. While the law again remains unclear in this area, Netiquette dictates that you request permission before linking to a site.

One final issue that you should be aware of with respect to linking is confusion of authorship. The linking of your learning materials to other sites may lead your learners to become confused as to who actually wrote, designed or developed the materials. This can be a violation of the original author's rights. Currently this problem can be overcome in the technical design of your learning materials or when building your Web server. A far more simple solution is not to do it in the first place. Make sure that your materials are clearly labelled and links correctly identified in ways that leave no doubt in the minds of your learners as to who the author is.

OBTAINING PERMISSION

In order to ensure that you do not infringe copyright you should, as part of the job of planning your learning materials, develop a request for permission letter ready for sending to various publishers.

Your letter should include the following information:

- the source of your material
- a complete bibliographic citation

Emphasize in your copyright request that the materials are going to be used in an educational, not-for-profit organization.

- for a book, the name of the author or authors, the title of the work, the city of publication, the publisher and the date
- for an article in a periodical, the name of the author or authors, the title of the article, the name of the periodical, the volume and number, the date and the pages of the article
- for an electronic source, the name of the author or authors, title of the document, title of the complete work (if applicable), document data or date of last revision (if different from access date), protocol and address, access path or directories (date of access)

(A number of different electronic style formats are in use at present. For a full listing, search under E-References or E-Citations on the World Wide Web.)

- a list of the page(s) you wish to reproduce
- the name of the learning event in which you are going to use the material and how many times a year the event will be presented
- how many learners will be using the materials.

Your letter should also request non-exclusive rights to the material for a minimum of two years in order to avoid having to request permission every time the event takes place. If you think you will not be revising your materials for a longer period of time then you may wish to request non-exclusive rights for up to three years (but do not expect to receive it).

It is important that you emphasize in your request that the materials are to be used in an event offered by a non-profit educational institution or in a not-for-profit learning event. Many authors and publishers charge either no fees or more reasonable fees when their work is being used for educational or learning purposes.

However, you should be aware that most requests for the use of comic strips, (many learning materials developers build in comic strips at the beginning of learning materials as ice breakers) will, most probably, not be granted or if they are, you will be asked to pay a substantial fee for each time that you use the materials. You should also be aware that some of the authors of the more popular comic strips have successfully won a number of law suits over the 'illegal' use of their materials.

Generally speaking, your copyright requests should be addressed to the publisher. Because the author has retained copyright in the material, the publisher will either notify you or forward your request to the author.

Figure 11.1 shows an example of a typical copyright letter. The text in bold indicates the information that you will need to complete.

Current date

Copyright holder's address

Dear Sir or Madam

It is our understanding that you control copyright for the following material:

materials citation

We would like to reproduce this material for use in **your course name**

Approximately **number of students** are expected to enrol in each session of the course, **when the course is offered**. We are requesting non-exclusive **your country name** rights to the material for **the amount of time for request.**

The **name of your department** at **name of your institution** offers a wide variety of courses in **what your institution does**.

If we may reproduce the material described above, please complete the enclosed permission form and return it to me at the address below or, if you prefer, submit your own contract.

We would appreciate your reply as soon as possible. If you prefer to respond by fax, the department's number is **your fax number**. Thank you for your consideration in this matter.

Sincerely

Your name, position, department and organization

Figure 11.1 *A typical copyright letter*

An example of a typical permission form is shown in Figure 11.2.

Permission for reproduction

Permission is granted to the **your department at your organization** to reproduce the following material for use during the next **time applied for and name of course**.

materials citation

Credit statement: _____

_____

_____

_____

_____

(If no credit statement is indicated, the bibliographic citation above will be used, followed by 'reproduced by permission'.)

Fee (if applicable): _____

Name (please print): _____

Position: _____

Signature: _____   Date: _____

Figure 11.2   *A typical permission form*

Again, the text in bold indicates the information that you will need to complete.

KEEPING TRACK OF YOUR COPYRIGHT REQUESTS

As you develop your learning materials you should keep a simple copyright log that notes publication data, requests and reply dates, whether or not permission has been granted, the fee (if any) and whether the fee has been paid. If a fee is requested, you would probably have to negotiate with someone in your organization about who pays it and how much is to be paid.

Several weeks before your course materials are to be printed, if you are using paper based materials, or before the materials are put up in an on-line environment, you should check to make sure all permission forms have been received. If there are any that have not arrived you should call the publisher and repeat your request over the phone. When verbal permission is given you should re-send the written request either through the post or fax. You may also wish to consider e-mail but it should be followed up by a letter or fax. This will complete your files and avoid any problems later.

Once you have received permission to use the materials, it is essential that you indicate this somewhere in the first pages of the material before it is reproduced. The most appropriate source statement is generally the complete bibliographic citation, copied from your request letter, followed by the phrase 'reproduced by permission'. If the copyright holder specifies a particular credit statement or credit line this must be reproduced exactly in your learning materials.

CONCLUSION

The issues of copyright may seem somewhat confusing. However, one way or the other copyright must be made part of both your materials planning and materials development phase of the work. While the issues of copyright are complex, the key to copyright matters is quite simple. Assume everything is either copyrighted or copyrightable and ask permission before you use the materials. Begging forgiveness later in a court of law usually won't work.

Chapter 12
Bringing It All Together

SUMMARY

This chapter brings together all of the various bits and pieces that makes the development of learning materials work for you.

This book is about planning how you are going to put together sound learning materials that the learner can use to help themselves learn. The first part of this process begins with reflections on a wide variety of issues essential to the overall success of the project. The process then continues with the development of the Course Information Document. This is followed by the development of the course profile and sub-profile to give you a complete overview of the various skills the learner will have to master in order to complete the course. Once this is done you then have to make some very difficult decisions regarding how the materials will be delivered to the learners. Finally, evaluation. It's possible that by placing a discussion on evaluation at the end of a book like this, the myth that evaluation is the last thing that you think about is being perpetuated. Nothing, of course, could be further from the truth. Chapter 1 will help you understand that evaluation must be considered up-front.

It is important that when you start a project that you start by dividing it into its distinct parts and phases

WHERE DO I START?

Chapter 1 divided the design and development of learning materials into four distinct parts or phases:

1. the gathering of information that will help you determine the focus and the priorities for the work you will be doing
2. the aims, objectives and sequence of the materials and the development of evaluative strategies so you can determine how all the materials worked in terms of the learning taking place
3. how well they stood the test in terms of format, layout and packaging
4. the production of the materials themselves, where you have to determine such things as page format and how it's all going to fit together.

A number of questions are posed in the chapter to help you reflect on matters essential to the job being completed on time and to budget. As you consider each of the questions you will need to think about the people you should engage to help you. These people should include instructional designers, writers, graphic artists and editors. Soliciting their help from the beginning rather than when things have gone wrong will, of course, help you get the job done on time and to budget, not to mention helping you to keep your sanity.

The key to understanding Chapter 1 is first to realize that the questions can be adapted to suit the job you have been asked to do. Second is to realize that all the work you put into answering the questions should be turned into documentation that will help you in both your decision making and in keeping the wolves at bay if something goes wrong. Keep a diary (as well as your appointment book) to record the various events that take place and the time taken for each event. This way you will find the next job that much easier to plan, budget and staff.

HOW DO I DETERMINE WHAT I REALLY NEED?

The second chapter, on developing the CID, discussed the need for the development of the documentation you will need to get the job completed. Again, a series of questions was suggested, this time to help you focus on the course and the materials themselves so you can get a picture of what the final product might look like.

The questions were placed into a number of categories, including who the materials are being planned for, why the materials are being developed in the first place and what the goals and aims are. It was noted that those responding to such questions would find them difficult to answer simply because they had never been asked to consider

Developing the CID is important as it provides the foundation for the development of your learning materials.

this kind of question before. These questions are important because they allow you to get a good sense of what is going on with the course, how people feel about them and what they mean to them. (Keep that diary handy!)

Flippant, off-hand responses, just like serious, reflective ones, tell you a great deal about the person, how they feel about the materials and the job you are doing. They will also give you some idea of the success you are going to have with the project and may give you cause to go about things in an entirely different way.

The second series of questions suggested in the chapter deals with what is to be included as part of the materials, how they are to be evaluated and how they will be used to deliver the message to the learner. Nuts and bolts questions, easy to answer? Yes and no. Yes, they are nuts and bolts questions but no, they are not easy to answer.

These questions are directed at you but few developers of learning materials have the courage to ask themselves these questions because to answer them in a meaningful way is to move into the unknown.

This is your opportunity to start thinking about doing something different. Look at the topics being considered and think of the different ways they can be delivered to the learner, and at the same time consider the different ways you can determine what and how much has been learned. Is a series of lectures with an examination at the end the only way to go, or can you get the learners to do something else that will enhance their learning? The key is to be adventurous, to push the limits, but remember to do it within the bounds of yourself, your learners and your institution.

The final part of the chapter discusses that much-forgotten part of planning and developing learning materials: determining the infrastructure needed to support what you are going to be doing in the classroom and, once the materials are developed, checking them out to see if they work in either a 'real' or simulated environment. Finally, the discussion touches on the idea of checking to see if the materials about to be developed already exist so you don't have to develop them over again.

Making the project run on time and on budget can only be achieved if you have a good plan.

MAKING IT ALL RUN SMOOTHLY

With all of this documentation and reflection behind you, the next phase of the development process, described in Chapter 3, should be relatively straightforward. The chapter provides you with the fundamentals of planning the work you are going to have to complete and determining what products will be produced. However, it's at this stage of the project you will possibly face your first major problem: that of trying to convince people that the work can't be completed by next week and that you will need time if the job is to be done properly.

Your second biggest problem will be getting the work completed on time and, therefore, to budget. Because of a lack of knowledge, many learning materials development projects start too late. This, of course, puts you in a difficult position because then it's really hard to convince people that a reasonable time is needed.

The key is that you should not be lulled into believing that you can do the job in less time than it should actually take. Throwing large amounts of resources at the job will not always work either. If time is just short, you may want to consider extra resources, but be careful as this takes planning and organization to make it work to your advantage and could lead to going over budget. If time is very short, you may want to consider extra resources and fast tracking in some way by having a number of events happening simultaneously. For example, you could start developing treatment plans based on the CID or the unvalidated profile. Or you might want to start resolving some of the inherent copyright problems based on what is outlined in the profile and sub-profile and at the same time start editing and proofreading materials as each page is completed, rather than wait until they are all finished. A number of other fast track options will also be available to you depending on the particular project. But be warned, this kind of fast tracking is difficult to co-ordinate and you can end up doing more work than normal. If you have to use this method then you will be wise to ensure that your work flowchart outlines all of the tasks being completed at the same time along with a date and sign-off for each.

If the time available to you is impossibly short you may have only two options open to you. The first is to start the project but only after you have made sure that all the documentation on the time problem is completed. The second is not to start the project at all.

DEVELOPING THE LEARNER PROFILE

The development of the learner profile discussed in Chapter 4 is your first view of all the materials you will be developing over the life of the project. You might ask why the task analysis and the subsequent time line are completed before the profile is determined. Remember that you should have enough information from the CID to be able to determine what needs to be done, develop your final products list and estab-

The learner profile provides you with the basis for your project plan and the materials you are developing.

lish your time lines. If you feel that some minor adjustments are needed in your time lines then they can be made after the profile is finalized. Because the profile and sub-profile take up considerable resources it is in your best interest to make sure that they are included in the overall project. Try not to put yourself in the position where you have to complete the profile first then, based on the profile, determine all of the resources you will need for the rest of the project. The only time this will work is if the project is in two parts and separate budgets and time lines have been developed for each.

Points to remember when developing the profile include making sure that the profile group goes as far as it can. Go over the materials with them as many times as possible until you are absolutely sure that they are right. Make sure that you know how the learner is to complete each of the tasks listed in the profile. Use verbs to help you try to ensure that each task is a measurable one for example, 'the learner should be able to appraise something' rather than 'the learner should be able to appreciate something'. Finally, make sure that you validate the profile to ensure that it is correct.

DEVELOPING THE LEARNER SUB-PROFILE

The sub-profile helps you better understand the component parts of the materials you are developing.

The sub-profile discussed in Chapter 5 helps you break down each of the learner tasks into their component parts. This is important for you and the writers/developers of the learning materials. You will need the detail to help you determine what has to be developed and what must be included in the materials. Points to remember here include making sure that the way the sub-profile is developed is an appropriate one. If you make the decision to develop it outside of the main profile group, that's fine. But if you decide that you are going to develop it during the main profiling session and at the last minute change your mind, make sure that you have a back-up plan to get it done another way.

DELIVERY OPTIONS: INSTRUCTIONAL STRATEGIES AND MATERIALS

Choosing the right delivery method for the materials you have designed is very important, so give it a lot of thought.

Chapter 6 focuses on the various factors you will have to consider in the choice of delivery strategies and methods for the materials you are developing. The choices are based on the size of the group you are dealing with and the environment in which the learning events are to take place. As noted earlier, it might be time to break out of that traditional lecture pattern and do something different. Remember, however, that if you do something different you may have to allow for extra time for the learning event as the learners will have to be 'trained' to do whatever it is that you want them to do. The chapter outlines three typical scenarios that can help you understand the choices that have to be made in this area. The chapter culminates with a description of learning materials and the range of choices available to you to make the learning experience a viable one for the learners.

CAN I REDESIGN THE MATERIALS I HAVE NOW?

Chapter 7 discusses the redesign of learning materials. Two possible scenarios come to mind here. The first is that if you followed the advice given in Chapter 2 you will have looked around and possibly found materials that you could use but they need some redesign and/or redevelopment. The second is that your present learning materials need updating. The chapter describes how you will need to develop documentation in the same way as you would when starting the development of new materials. The discussion then turns to the tasks that will need to be carried out if the redevelopment is to be a success. One of the major problems with redesign is the desire to go too far and do more than is necessary so that a 'new' product is developed, which took longer to develop because you had to dismantle the old one first.

Sometimes the redesign of materials can be more costly than starting from scratch, so factor that into your plans.

HOW DO I ASSESS THE LEARNERS *AND* EVALUATE THE LEARNING MATERIALS?

In Chapter 8 the discussion centres around the evaluation of the learner and the learning materials and how the evaluation can be reported to those who need such a report. The chapter poses a number of questions regarding formal and informal assessment, the place of each and when each needs to occur. What you must remember here is that the question of evaluation must be decided at the beginning of the project. This way the design and development of general goals and objectives and specific learner objectives become much easier to determine.

Develop your plan(s) for evaluating both the learning and the learning materials at the beginning of the project rather than at the end.

The learning materials themselves have to be evaluated to ensure that the role for which they were designed was correct. The development of this evaluation scheme must also be determined up-front. The report and the audience for that report also have to be established as this is important to both the learner and those funding the project.

The chapter continues with a discussion and description of those items that have to be considered for budget purposes. Budgets can be difficult to prepare, as some of you will discover. The problem with budgets is that they have to be accurate; if you don't budget for enough funds and resources, too bad, you live with the consequences, and if the budget is too high, the project isn't funded. When preparing your budget try to work closely with the funding agency – you can't afford not to – and make sure that the time you will need to complete the job is accounted for. Use the guidelines suggested in Chapter 1 to help you here. Make sure you have all of your contingency funds in place and, finally, make sure that all of your funds are accounted for as the project proceeds. Get the authority to advance funds for various expenses to one person in the team or keep that authority yourself and use a simple running or remaining balance accounting system to track outgoing funds.

WRITING LEARNING OBJECTIVES

This chapter describes the development of learning objectives. Once the learner profile and sub-profile is complete each of the learner tasks or competencies will need to be written as measurable general or specific learning objectives. The development of learning objectives is a relatively simple task, as long as you remember that the objective must be measurable. While we might want our learners to understand or appreciate something, it is difficult, if not impossible, to measure understanding or appreciation.

What you have to remember when writing your learning objectives is how you want your learners to show you that they understand what they have learned by doing something. This chapter helps you write measurable learning objectives.

WRITING TEST ITEMS

The writing of test items can be both a difficult and onerous task and is often relegated to the end of the materials design cycle. However, this should not be the case. Testing should be an objective procedure by which the performance of the learner is sampled and evaluated against a predetermined standard.

ISSUES OF COPYRIGHT

Chapter 11 looks at the issues of copyright and how these issues affect the planning process. The chapter defines copyright and reviews typical copyright infringement. The chapter also describes some of the problems with URLs, Web sites and linking your learning materials to a Web site. The chapter concludes with an overview of how you should go about obtaining copyright from an author.

It is hoped that the preceding discussion has brought all of the threads together so that you can systematically design and develop learning materials for your learners.

Further Reading

Briggs, L J, Gustafson, K L and Tillman, M H, (eds), (1991) *Instructional Design. Principles and Applications*, 2nd edn, Englewood Cliffs, NJ: Educational Technology Publications.

Dick, W and Reiser, R A (1989) *Planning Effective Instruction*, London: Allyn and Bacon.

Earl, T (1987) *The Art and Craft of Course Design*, London: Kogan Page.

Ebel, R L and Frisbie, D A (1991) *Essentials of Educational Measurement*, 5th edn, Englewood Cliffs, NJ: Prentice-Hall.

Einsiedel, A A (1984) *Improving Project Management*, Boston, Mass.: International Human Resources.

Ellington, H and Race, P (1992) *Producing Teaching Materials*, 2nd edn, London: Kogan Page.

Gagné, R M, Briggs, L J and Wager, W W (1992) *Principles of Instructional Design*, 4th edn, London: Harcourt Brace Jovanovich.

Gaynor, A K and Evanson, J L (1992) *Project Planning*, Boston, Mass.: Simon & Schuster.

Gentry, C G (1994) *Introduction to Instructional Development: Process and Technique*, Belmont, Ca: Wadsworth Publishing Company.

Goad, T W (1982) *Delivering Effective Training*, San Diego, Ca: University Associates.

Greer, M (1992) *ID Project Management: Tools and Techniques for Instructional Designers and Developers*, Englewood Cliffs, NJ: Educational Technology Publications.

Grunland, N E (1976) *Measurement and Evaluation in Teaching*, New York: Macmillan.

Grunlund, N E (1978) *Stating Objectives for Classroom Instruction*, 2nd edn, London: Collier Macmillan.

Hartley, J (1994) *Designing Instructional Text*, London: Kogan Page.

Kliem, R L and Ludin, I S (1993) *The Noah Project: The secrets of practical project management*, Aldershot: Gower.

Lester, A (1992) *Project Planning and Control*, 2nd edn, Oxford: Butterworth-Heinemann.

Mager, R F (1975) *Preparing Instructional Objectives*, Belmont, California: Pitman Learning.

Reigeluth, C M (ed.) (1987) *Instructional Theories In Action*, London: Lawrence Erlbaum.

Romiszowski, A J (1984) *Producing Instructional Systems*, London: Kogan Page.

Rowntree, D (1990) *Teaching through self-instruction*, revised edn, London: Kogan Page.

Sax, G (1980) *Principles of Educational and Psychological Measurement* (2nd edn), Belmont, Ca: Wadsworth.

Wilson, B (1987) *Methods of Training: Groupwork*, volume 2, Training technology programme, Carnforth: Parthenon Publishing.

Wilson, B (1987) *Methods of Training and Individualised Instruction*, volume 3, Training technology programme, Carnforth: Parthenon Publishing.

Index